Organizing Paper @Home: What to Toss and How to Find the Rest

To Jill —
Love working with
you — I am blessed!
Barbara

by
BARBARA HEMPHILL
with
JENNIFER WIG

Raleigh, NC, USA

Acknowledgements

This book would not have occurred without the valuable support of the following people:

My co-author, Jennifer Wig, with whom it has been sheer joy to write this book, and to whom I've given the title "Keeper of the Legacy."

My parents, Everett and Doris Frost, who role-modeled the principles that have been the basis of my business for 30+ years.

My husband, Alfred Taylor, who says his job is to "block and tackle so you can fly." No words can express my love and gratitude!

My best friend, Florence Feldman, who told me 28 years ago "I believe in you," and who helped me launch the first edition of this book in 1988!

My business partner, Andrea Anderson. We call each other "Peanut Butter" and "Jelly" – and those of you who have worked with us know why!

The CPES (Certified Productive Environment Specialist) Community, who continually serve as motivation to keep improving the products and services we offer.

And of course, the clients and audiences whom I have had the pleasure to serve since 1978. I am indeed blessed by all of you!

Table of Contents

Introduction

I first shared my dream of writing this book with my lifelong friend and colleague Florence Feldman in 1981. Her professional expertise and personal friendship become more valuable to me as the years go by.

It is amazing that 23 years have passed since the first edition of Taming the Paper Tiger was published by Dodd, Mead. It is even more amazing that the problem of paper continues to be the No. 1 organizing challenge in the household! The computer was touted as being the tool to eliminate paper from our lives and enabled us to be more organized. In many ways, it did, but it also allowed us to generate more paper than ever before, and we learned that organizing electronic files has its own challenges!

The reality of "paperless" has not happened, and I personally promote the concept of "almost paperless" – since in some instances, paper is simply a more practical and/or desirable format. In addition to the fact we have more paper and more computers, life seems to get more complicated in every way every day – and much of that complexity is reflected in both realms.

In my continuing experience as a productivity consultant, I have observed that the principles, practices, and techniques I espoused in the first edition of Taming the Paper Tiger are still true: "Only the names have changed," as the familiar expression states. Hence, it seemed appropriate to publish a new edition of this book designed to be relevant in today's digital world. One of the key components of my life philosophy is "Together We Are Better." With that in mind, I invited Jennifer Wig to partner with me in writing this new edition – and what a joy it has been. I know that you, the reader, will benefit too, and my hope is that because of her insight and contribution, the principles, practices and techniques in this book will last another 30 years!

I am especially thankful for the love and support of my husband, Alfred Taylor, who is the greatest fan club any writer ever had, and with whom I enjoy my life more every day. Happy paper organizing!

Chapter One
The Roar of a New Tiger

When I first wrote this book, computers were just starting to become part of the home office scene and more often than not, were creating more paper than they saved. Today, it is completely different. People are lounging on their couches with iPads, making notes and sending emails from their smartphones, and handling most aspects of their daily lives with the help of a computer.

Does this sound familiar? You're paying some bills online at your desk, but you realize you need to save a copy of one of the bills to keep for tax reasons. Didn't you create a file for that purpose? Where is it saved? Medical bills – in paper form – are arriving each day from your hospital stay last year, with some of them payable online and some must be paid via snail mail. What to do with that stack of paper and how to organize that and the electronic files? In the middle of this musing, your son comes in and asks for a copy of something for school, but the printer ink is dried up because you're not using it as much. Then your cell phone rings, and it's your friend asking if you want to go shopping the 18th. Your electronic calendar tracking both work and home appointments says you're free, but you have the nagging feeling that you're missing something. Did you write it down on a Gmail task list? Or in your handy little "old-fashioned" notebook?

The roar of the paper tiger is ever present in our daily lives – even when our lives are stored in computer files instead of filing cabinets. Did you know that one of top requests from Hewlett Packard for any electronic device is the ability to print?

A computer is like any other tool: Use it correctly and it can help, but otherwise it's just a large paperweight of metal and plastic. It can either save you from wading through paper or create more problems than ever. And as we blend our lives more and more with computers, it can be hard to remember where to find the item you need.

As an organizing consultant, I've spent thousands of hours working with people and their paper, from parents struggling with the piles of papers their kids bring home from school, to corporate executives responsible for thousands of files. One fact remains absolutely clear: paper-management skills are essential to survive the information explosion in our society.

A Slow Change

In 1926, a little more than 15,000 pieces of mail were sent nationwide. By 2000, we were sending more than 207.5 billion pieces of mail per year. But now, that figure is declining, down to 171 billion in 2010.

Pingdom, a firm that watches the Web, estimates that in 2009, 90 trillion e-mails were sent – that's 247 billion email messages a day! Those figures are expected to grow. In 2010, the number of people worldwide using email was about 1.9 million. That's expected to reach 2.5 billion by 2014, according to Radicati Group, Inc.

Also worth noting: In 2001, spam accounted for an estimated 5 percent of our email. By 2007, it clogged our inboxes, accounting for 90-95 percent of all email sent.

People often say they hate paper and thus, they hate dealing with emails and files as well. But if that's true, why do they have so much trouble clicking "delete" or getting rid of it? How many people still print out that important e-mail message—or the information gathered from a great website? Computers have an increasing impact on our lives; learning to manage the paper and files they generate is essential.

How many emails are sitting in your inbox? Or in other email folders? Those cute forwards from your sister-in-law, the reminder to pay your credit card bill, the email from your rental house about your upcoming trip – the list just seems to keep growing! It may not be taking up space on your kitchen counter, but the overwhelming feeling generated by all that electronic paper remains.

Your ability to accomplish any task is directly related to your ability to find the right thing at the right time.

No matter what changes are occurring, paper is still the No. 1 organizing challenge for most households. Paper junk mail continues to invade our lives. You may not get a real card in the mail for your birthday anymore, but you're still inundated with catalogs, magic money-making offers, advertisements, and even some bills and business items that just haven't yet made the jump to paperless.

Most people know how to do most of the individual tasks required in personal paper or e-paper management—-paying bills, writing letters, creating files, etc. The difficult part is getting it all done at the right time. To accomplish that requires a comprehensive system.

This book provides guidelines to help you fill in the gaps in your paper management system, or to develop a totally new one if you feel it's necessary. And, since we're dealing with both paper and e-files, the principles I discuss apply to both worlds.

Developing a personal paper-management system takes motivation, time, and practice. If you've been shuffling the same documents and files for months, or even years, it will take time to change, and it can be frightening. Accept this as a "normal" reaction, not an indication that you are doing something wrong.

Digging through a pile of papers or a folder full of old Word documents can be likened to waking a sleeping tiger. We discover documents that represent disappointments, obligations, uncertainty, indecision and the blinding reality that we are not able to do all the things we want to or think we ought to.

Just as we have a temporary respite when the tiger sleeps, we have a temporary respite when we ignore the papers — with the fear that the tiger will awake at any moment constantly in the back of our minds.

Chapter Two
Roar Right Back

With the invention of computers arrived this excitement that we could "go paperless" in our offices and even our homes. What most people found, however, is that these computers only added to the paper piles. We were adding printing and photocopying to our massive stack of papers and saw no signs of slowing down.

Things have changed. But if you think you're going to go paperless, hold on minute. At this point, it's still not possible. What? Barbara, that's why I bought this - I thought I could.

Nope. The day will come when the technology will make totally paperless an option, but we're not there yet.

> Four Questions to Ask About Every Piece of Paper and/or Computer Document:
> 1. Do I really need to keep this?
> 2. Where should I keep it?
> 3. How long should I keep it?
> 4. How can I find it?

I am here to help you go Almost Paperless.™ You might read your newspaper online, but you don't own a tablet or don't want to read your magazines in that format. There's still junk mail showing up in your mailbox. And some records, documents and other items simply must be kept on paper.

For example, I recently met with the CEO of a company who joined the board of a local non-profit organization. The first thing he received was a three-inch binder of documents pertinent to the organization. Scanning through all of the documents is not really practical – or even necessary — so keeping the binder is the best option. The day will come when the organization will have an electronic notebook, making the binder unnecessary, with significant savings for both the environment and office.

So this book is here to help you go Almost Paperless™ and to manage both your paper and electronic files. Sound overwhelming? Don't worry. In general, when you see the word "paper" in these paragraphs, you can usually interchange it with "computer files" or "computer documents." The basic principles of managing your paper – electronic or hard copies – remain the same.

Let's get started.

First, paper and file management means developing a system that fits your personal needs. No matter what your file management challenges are, there's a way for you to improve the way you handle paper—one that you create yourself for your own particular needs and lifestyle. You may know how to handle a particular file problem, but for various reasons, you have not done so. Before long, the file gets lost in the shuffle of more files and folders. You become so bogged down in all your various spreadsheets and word documents ... and yes, even your paper, that you end up not taking the appropriate action to end the vicious cycle.

Successful file management requires five basic ingredients:
1. Clear picture of desired results
2. Positive attitude
3. Sufficient time
4. Appropriate tools
5. Regular maintenance

If any component of the system is weak or missing, the system will begin to break down. Nine times out of ten, when a system breaks down, it is a sign of a changing situation, not a bad system. Perhaps the numbers of papers/files have grown, the support system has changed, or the objectives have been revised.

A Clear Picture

The first question I frequently ask a client is "What would success look like?" or "What will you be able to do when you are organized that you are not doing now?" Organization in and of itself has no value—it is simply a tool to help you do what you want to do. The clearer you are about what you want to do, the more effectively you can get organized.

Paper itself is not the problem. Paper is a symptom of a problem.

Getting organized is not about becoming a neat freak—unless, of course, you want to—or about doing things the way someone else does. My definition of organization is very simple: Does it work? Do you like it? If what you organize (or don't organize) affects others, then you should ask a third question, "Does it work for others?"

Think Positively

A positive attitude as it relates to paper management is an essential prerequisite. It is important for you to expect that, with the help of this book, you can and will develop a system for yourself that will suit your particular needs.

One of the most exciting aspects of being an organizing consultant is helping people create a system to fit their specific needs, and then seeing their sense of relief when they realize how much simpler their lives can be. Frequently, people procrastinate doing anything about the disorganization in their lives because they are waiting to find the "right" way.

There is no "right" or "wrong" way! Many times I set up systems for other people that I personally would find very frustrating. As you read this book you will discover that there are many styles of paper or file management. Don't worry about how other people do it. Just look for techniques that work for you. What you do with a piece of paper is not nearly as important as doing it consistently.

To foster your positive attitude about file management, recognize that any system you develop is a tool to help you do what you want or need to do. A friend of mine says, "I hate jogging; I love having jogged!" Paperwork and file management is like that in many ways. Few people, if any, like doing it, but taking the time to set up a system means spending less time shuffling through it all and more time enjoying the results.

Tomorrow Never Arrives

How many times have you said to yourself: "I'll get organized when things calm down/after I write the report for my boss/when the kids go back to school/when the kids get out of school/after the guests leave/when I come home from my business trip/when the house is remodeled/as soon as I have a block of time — this weekend maybe, or over the holidays/when I'm on vacation/when I retire/tomorrow."

The weekend, the holidays, the vacations come and go. As soon as one crisis is over (and sometimes even before!), another begins. And the cycle continues. Before you know it, you have an inbox full of e-mails you really intended to answer and 10 months of health insurance claims to submit. The desk at your office is covered with memos unfiled and business journals unread. The attic and basement are filled with magazines that never got read while they were in the den (but that contain wonderful articles and recipes). Plus, it's April 10th, and you have no idea where your receipts are stashed. Many a client has called after being retired for several months, or even years, saying "I still don't have the time."

If you wait "until things calm down" before you do something about the paper in your life, it could be a very long wait.

Decide to Decide

There is a very simple axiom regarding paper: Paper clutter is postponed decisions; paper management is making decisions. Papers pile up on our counters, tables and desks because there are decisions we need to make about them. "Do I really need to keep this letter from my lawyer about my father's estate?" "Where should I keep my will?" "What do I do with all those family photographs my mother gave me for safekeeping?" "Should I keep that online recipe saved somewhere?" "What should I do with health insurance statements?" "Where do I put the operating instructions for the new garage door opener?"

Paper itself is not the problem. Paper is a symptom of the problem. Every time you ask one of the above questions without making a decision—a reply—and then taking the appropriate action, you have left some unsettled business. Postpone a few of the decisions, and a new pile is born.

Six Information Management Questions to Ask About Every Piece of Paper/Computer Document:

1. Do I really need to keep this?
2. In what format?
3. For how long?
4. Who is responsible for filing it?
5. Who needs access to it?
6. How can I find it?

Each of these questions requires making a decision. But many people run into trouble here. Why are these decisions so difficult for us to make? There are two major reasons—lack of information and fear of failure.

Information, Please

Even though paper management is an essential skill in the 21st century, few people have had an opportunity to learn these skills in a formal way. It simply is not taught.

The purpose of this book is to help you recognize the paper-management problems in your life, to motivate you to do something about them, and to provide you with the tools to find solutions and develop systems.

The place to begin this process is with the scorecard at the end of this chapter. I developed it as the starting point for my clients.

By completing the scorecard, you'll identify the areas of paper/file management you believe are your weak spots. Any score of 3 or higher indicates you could use some help in that area.

You do not need to read the entire book to be able to put it to work for you, but read an entire chapter before you begin trying a new system. Use this as a reference book, not only when you are first setting up a system, but also to refer to as you outgrow existing systems and find you need to make revisions.

But ... What If?

Fear is a big reason people have difficulty deciding what to do with their papers. You're afraid that your decision will be proven wrong, you'll regret your decision, or that someone will be disappointed or hurt by your decision. You ask yourself: "What if I get audited by the IRS and I don't have what I need?" "What if I throw something away and it turns out to be very valuable?" "What if my children want or need this information someday?" "What if I file this important document and then I can't find it?"

It's not easy to answer the "what-ifs" correctly. Most of us have, at one time or another, thrown out something we wound up needing later on. Here are the facts: 1) If your paper problem is big enough, you can't find most of your paper anyway; and 2) Almost everything is replaceable. You can probably get another copy if you really need to, and, if you don't really need to, then it probably wasn't worth the clutter it would have caused in the first place.

Here's what I call Hemphill's Principle: "If you don't know you have it, or you can't find it, it is of NO value to you!"

No Magic in Insight

Suppose you can take the time to set up a system, and you know what you need to do, but you just don't want to do it? What then?

There is no magic in insight! Just because you know there is a better way, doesn't mean you will do it. You need to take action on your insight. I know that if I exercise at least 20 minutes a day, three times a week, I will feel better, look better and live longer—but that in itself does not make me ride my bicycle or go for a jog.

In fact, we frequently do not act on our insights—until a crisis forces us to do so. We become concerned about our eating habits when the doctor says our life is at risk if we do not. Similarly, we decide to do something about a cluttered desk when we recognize that it doesn't work for us anymore. One client decided to do something about his paper tiger when the penalty on his overdue inheritance-tax bill became larger than his annual income and he was threatened with jail! What price are you willing to pay before you act?

Ultimately, you will have to make the decision to tame the tiger yourself. The most I can do is point out how chaotic the alternative is and show you ways to create a system that works for you. No doubt you know that already, or you wouldn't be reading this. This book will give you answers to questions and guidelines to use that will help you create your own system for managing the paper in your life. The rest is up to you.

Try filling out our Productive Environment Scorecard to show you in which areas you need the most help. You can also fill this out online at https://productiveenvironment.wufoo.com/forms/productive-environment-scorecard-for-individuals.

Paper Management Skills Survey
When I meet with a new client, the first thing I do is ask the client to fill out this questionnaire to determine what areas of paper management need work. Answer the questions yourself. Any question that gets a 3 or higher indicates an area where you need help. The right-hand column tells which chapter to turn to.

Strongly Agree = 1   Agree = 2   Uncertain = 3   Disagree = 4   Strongly Disagree = 5

Issue	Rating	See Chapter
I have an accessible and comfortable place in my home where I do paperwork.	1 2 3 4 5	3
I have the "paper-management tools" (paper, office supplies, etc.,) that I need.	1 2 3 4 5	3
I have a calendar system that works for me and my family.	1 2 3 4 5	9
I can easily find names, addresses and phone numbers when I need them.	1 2 3 4 5	12
I have a bill-paying system that works for me.	1 2 3 4 5	14
I have a filing system that works for me, and can be used by others if necessary.	1 2 3 4 5	13
I can find family records (medical, educational, etc.) whenever I need them.	1 2 3 4 5	19

I am comfortable with my record of charitable donations.	1 2 3 4 5	13
I am confident my tax records are adequate for the IRS.	1 2 3 4 5	16
I keep good records of household and automobile repairs and maintenance.	1 2 3 4 5	13
I have a large wastebasket/recycle bin I can reach when doing my paperwork.	1 2 3 4 5	3
I can find warranties and directions for appliances when I need them.	1 2 3 4 5	13
I am comfortable with my records of magazine and newspaper subscriptions.	1 2 3 4 5	17
I am comfortable with the newspapers and magazines around my house.	1 2 3 4 5	17
I like the way my recipes are organized.	1 2 3 4 5	21
I have enough space for books, and can find one when I want or need it.	1 2 3 4 5	3, 17
I organize my photographs and other family memorabilia to my satisfaction.	1 2 3 4 5	20
I can easily reach the telephone when I am working.	1 2 3 4 5	3
I am comfortable with the amount of time I spend retrieving information.	1 2 3 4 5	11
I can find the information I called about when my phone call is returned.	1 2 3 4 5	11
I have a "To Do" list system that works for me.	1 2 3 4 5	10
I take some action on a piece of paper every time I pick it up.	1 2 3 4 5	7
I am comfortable with the amount of paper I throw away or recycle.	1 2 3 4 5	8
I keep up with my correspondence to my satisfaction.	1 2 3 4 5	18
I can find travel information or records whenever I want them.	1 2 3 4 5	23
I am comfortable with the way I handle my children's records and memorabilia.	1 2 3 4 5	22
I could find the papers I want to take with me if I had to evacuate my house.	1 2 3 4 5	19
I pay my bills on time.	1 2 3 4 5	11, 14

Chapter Three
Get Centered

Here is a funny story from an anonymous forwarded e-mail:

I have recently been diagnosed with AAADD - Age Activated Attention Deficit Disorder. This is how it goes:

I decide to wash the car, start toward the garage and notice the mail on the table. OK, I'm going to wash the car...

BUT FIRST I'm going to go through the mail. Lay car keys down on desk. After discarding the junk mail, I notice the trashcan is full. OK, I'll just put the bills on my desk....

BUT FIRST I'll take the trash out, but since I'm going to be near the mailbox, I'll address a few bills.... Yes, now where is the checkbook? Oops... there's only one check left. Where did I put the extra checks? Oh, there's my empty plastic cup from last night on my desk. I'm going to look for those checks...

BUT FIRST I need to put the cup back in the kitchen. I head for the kitchen, look out the window, notice the flowers need a drink of water, I put the cup on the counter and there's my extra pair of glasses on the kitchen counter. What are they doing here? I'll just put them away...

BUT FIRST, need to water those plants. I head for the door and... Aaaagh! Someone left the TV remote in the wrong spot. Okay, I'll put the remote away and water the plants...

BUT FIRST I need to find those checks.

END OF DAY: Car not washed, bills still unpaid, cup still in the sink, checkbook still has only one check left, lost my car keys; and, when I try to figure out why nothing got done today, I'm baffled because... I KNOW I WAS BUSY ALL DAY! I realize this condition is serious... I'd get help... BUT FIRST... I think I'll check my e-mail.

That story illustrates one of the biggest problems in getting things done – getting centered. It can be a challenge – even if you're not diagnosed with ADD or ADHD (as I have been, by the way) – because there is always so much to do.

If you want to tame that paper tiger, you have to start by putting him in a cage. So the first step in solving your paper/file management (aka life management) problem is to get centered – literally. You need to choose one place in your home as your Business Center.

At seminars I give for managing paper at the office, one of the most frequent comments I hear from participants is, "It's even worse at home!" I ask them, "Where do you do your paperwork at home?" Typically, the response is, "Sometimes here . . . sometimes there."

Therein lies a major part of the problem! It fascinates me that nearly everyone has a specific location in their home devoted to the preparation of food. Many fewer people have a specific location devoted to the handling of paper and the business of life. Yet most people spend as much or more time handling life's business than they do preparing food!

Just taking your mail to a central place will eliminate scattered piles of paper, misplaced bills and checks, and forgotten notices. One class participant was amazed at how much easier her life became once she established a work area in the kitchen with a desk, a telephone and a filing cabinet.

Maybe you already have a location, but it's covered in paper! Or maybe you're so used to being mobile that you carry your laptop and smartphone with you all over the house. Even if that's the case, I strongly urge you to set up a permanent center for your work that will be available to you at all times.

"How can that be so important?" you may ask. Have you ever tried to fix something with your fingernails or hands because you didn't feel like going to the basement to get the proper tool? Have you ruined a jacket trying to remove a spot on your suit without the proper cleaner? Have you ever mailed a birthday card a week later than you planned to because you kept forgetting to buy stamps?

When I was a child growing up on a Nebraska farm, my father used to tell me that half the battle in getting any job done is having the right tool. The same is true in paper management. In my experience, every household needs what I call a "Home Office for the Business of Life."

Choose Your Business Center

The first thing to consider in choosing a place for handling the business of life is a comfortable location. If you like sunshine or have allergies to mold, an unfinished, dark basement is not likely to be satisfactory. If you like to be in the mainstream of family activity, the family room may be an excellent location. Maybe you're easily distracted or you'd like a quiet place to go to after a hectic day at the office. Then an out-of-the-way bedroom or a study will probably work better. If you have small children, you could set up your work center in an area where they can play while you work.

While everyone has a specific location in their home devoted to the preparation of food, far fewer people have a specific location devoted to the handling of paper.

Paperwork under the best of circumstances isn't much fun, and you won't be encouraged to do it if you dislike your work area. So, do whatever you can to make it a place you like to be. Keep your mp3 player nearby if you like music. Put a cushion on your chair, or get a new lamp to put on your desk.

Many people would rather not set aside a separate space for a work area, preferring to use the kitchen or dining room table. Others have no option but to use these tables because of space constraints. In this case I recommend a mobile bill-paying center that can be housed in a portable file box, basket or rolling file. Check your local office supply store or try online for some examples. However, if at all possible, establish a permanent location that can be used exclusively for managing your stuff. You don't want to have to constantly interrupt the bill-paying process because the table has to be cleared and set for dinner.

A Desk Is a Desk

Is a Desk . . . Or Is It?

Does it matter what type of desk or desk arrangement you designate for your work center? You bet it does! Some desks simply do not work for you. The key word is "functional."

Have a laptop? Sure, the couch is a comfy place to work, but having a desk helps you be more productive. If nothing else, it gives you a place to keep the laptop when not in use.

Many people have desks that are lovely to look at and horrible to use. A rolltop desk, for example, while very beautiful, is difficult for most people to use because of the limited workspace, and the numerous cubbyholes soon become catch-alls for unidentified papers. If you are going to use such a desk, be sure to label the various compartments: one for envelopes, one for postcards, one for stamps, and so on.

Some people love those beautiful secretary desks—love to look at them, that is. The biggest disadvantage to this type of desk is its small size. Even if you're Almost Paperless™, you will still likely handle some paper, and need at least one file drawer. The best way to use a secretary is to designate it for a particular paper project, such as writing real paper letters. If you are particularly fond of the desk or it has sentimental significance, this will be an advantage. You will like to go there, and you will therefore be more inclined to write personal letters. Keep all your notepaper and stationery there, or at least a supply of any different styles you may use, as well as any greeting cards you have purchased.

Chances are, you need to make room for your computer on the desk. Have a laptop? Sure, the couch is a comfy place to work, but having a desk helps you be more productive. If nothing else, it gives you a place to keep the laptop when not in use. Don't make the mistake of using an outdated desk for the computer – in order to enjoy the task and avoid injury, your station should be ergonomically sound. The monitor needs to be at eye level and you need a keyboard tray. Laptop users can buy a docking station for their laptop, which allows for a bigger monitor (or more than one!) and full keyboard.

One of my clients had four desks and none of them worked. Her first assignment was to choose the one she liked most, get some boxes and empty it entirely. From that point, we started over to make not only a desk that she liked, but a desk that worked!

Obviously, many of the decisions you make regarding your work area will be based on how much room you have in your home. But there are many options – even if your space is limited.

To hold supplies such as stamps, paper, clips, pens, etc., consider buying a filing cabinet that has two small drawers and one file-depth drawer. You could also look in home- and office-organizing stores and online for a small drawer to install under the table top. (Drawers designed to fit under a kitchen cabinet might do very nicely.) Try a plastic caddy designed to carry tools or cleaning supplies, or get more decorative and pick up some small acrylic, wood or brass organizers. If you plan on using a computer at this homemade desk, you can find pull-out keyboard trays in many office supply stores.

Set Up Your Center
Wherever you choose to make your work area, be sure you have adequate lighting and a comfortable chair. One client and I spent a considerable amount of time setting

up her paper-management system. She understood it and liked it, yet she never seemed to get things done—until we discovered the root of the problem. Her arthritic neck always hurt when she sat at the desk. As soon as we purchased an adjustable chair, the neck ache disappeared. When adjusting your chair, most experts agree that you want both feet planted firmly on the floor and your keyboard at a level where your elbows are parallel to the floor.

If you want to be able to move around in your work area, you will find a swivel chair on rollers a big advantage. If there is carpeting, you will need an acrylic chair mat.

A major factor in managing paper is an effective filing system. (For detailed discussion, see Chapter 13.) A filing cabinet is one of the best investments you will ever make. It is ideal if your filing system is located at or close to your work center. For those who use very little paper, there is still some pouring in, and you will need at least one file drawer.

There is a variety of filing equipment on the market—other than the traditional metal filing cabinet—ranging from inexpensive cardboard boxes to costly acrylic cabinets on rollers. Rolling files are an excellent choice if you can't keep your files at your work area. You can move them to your work place as you need them and roll them back out of the way when you're done.

This is not an area to skimp – make sure your filing cabinet has full–extension drawers (some of the cheaper models do not). If you can't open the filing cabinet to its full extension, you will not be able to access the papers in the back, causing frustration, lost files and worst of all – a broken filing system. Most types of files are found in office-supply stores and online. You can also check in your online yellow pages or to see if there are "gently used office furniture stores" that sell great quality office equipment at affordable prices.

In these days of cell phones, many people don't keep a landline. If you don't, keep your cell phone with you at your desk while you work. If you do have a landline, bring your cordless phone over to the desk, because sometimes, you can immediately eliminate pieces of paper or tasks by making a phone call when you first open your mail.

Designate a special place to put those items that are ready to go to the mailbox or the post office. A napkin holder works well and can add to the personality of your workspace. I use a beautifully handcrafted ceramic one that I purchased on a vacation, which evokes pleasant memories each time I look at it.

You will also need a "To Sort" tray (see Chapter 7) located on or within easy reach of your desk to collect the papers that require your action when you are ready to deal with them.

You might find a calculator helpful, and your cell phone or computer already has one. However, if you prefer to use a hand-held one, be sure to keep it in your desk. Some people also love bulletin boards, but be careful! For many, it simply becomes a catchall for postponed decisions. To avoid that, identify it for a specific purpose, such as upcoming invitations, greeting cards, or other mementos you've received (to be changed when they become tired-looking) or messages to family members.

Last, but not least, a large trash can is one of the most important tools in your work area. I can't explain why, but I've observed that people are more likely to use a large trashcan than a small one, so choose carefully! If you generate a lot of recyclable paper, be sure to have two wastebaskets: a large one for the paper and a smaller one for incidental waste.

Basic Supplies

Once you have all the major equipment you need, concentrate on getting the necessary desk supplies. Nothing is more annoying than discovering you've run out of staples, or to find a bill you thought was paid a week ago buried in the bottom of your purse or briefcase because you didn't have a stamp when you needed it. You can order your stamps by mail or online from the post office. If you mail a lot of things, you might even buy a simple postal scale. You can then print your own stamps at www.stamps.com. (Learn more about online bill paying in Chapter 6.)

Be wary of clutter such as pens that don't write well, paperweights you don't like or use, or drawers full of forgotten objects. When was the last time you picked up that novelty pen and actually wrote something with it? If your desk is filled with things you don't use, start over! Get a box and empty the contents of your desk into them, keeping only those items you use or enjoy seeing in your work area.

Check the at the end of the chapter for a list of more work center tools.

If you have everything you feel you will need, the first step on the road to effective paper management is complete. Congratulations!

A Note About Sharing

Although our mothers taught us that sharing was an admirable thing, when it comes to a desk, it is seldom workable unless both partners are really willing to work at it. Sharing a desk requires communication, flexibility, and discipline. It's often easier and more effective to create a second workspace, giving the most desirable spot to the person who spends the most time at the desk.

An Office in a Closet

If you live in a small apartment, condominium or house, finding a place you can call your own to do paperwork may require some creative thinking. One client solved the problem by turning her front hall closet into an office so she could organize her paper as soon as she walked in the front door. She put in a small file cabinet, a large wastebasket, a bulletin board, and some "cubby holes" to sort her bills, reading material, filing etc. A counter-high table with a stool where she could sit to sort her mail completed the scene, and solved a problem she had struggled with for 20 years. The large double-door closets found in the bedrooms of many new homes work very well, and may be the perfect solution for you.

Checklist of Essential Tools and Supplies for Any Office

Here's a checklist of supplies no well-organized office or work area should be without. We'll discuss the importance of having the right tools later in the book, and certainly office supplies fall into that category. What happens when you clip a magazine article for your files, and when you go to staple it, and discover you are out of staples? You're frustrated. At that point you can make a special trip to get staples (a waste of time when you could have made one trip to pick up many supplies, avoiding lots of "special trips.") Or, you have to fold the corner together as a poor substitute for a staple (the pages fall apart). Wouldn't it be simpler to just make sure you have an extra box of staples?

•Telephone

• "In Box," for items you haven't looked at. Keep this space finite, when it is full you MUST pay attention to it; do not submit to the temptation of buying a bigger "in box."

• "Out Box," for items to be mailed or given to someone else.

•"To File Box," for items to be filed in drawers you can't reach from your chair.

•Container for writing utensils, unless you'd rather keep them in your drawer. In addition to pens and pencils, they should include:

    -Highlighter

    -Felt-tipped pen for handwriting file labels

    -Thick marker for marking boxes

    -Different colored pens for calendar notations if you use a paper calendar

•Address book, unless you keep that information electronically

•Calendar (paper or electronic)

•Stapler, staples and staple remover

•Labelmaker (worth considering for files, shelves and doors)

•Clock (if you don't use your cell phone or computer clock)

•Ruler

•Magnifying glass, if you need to read very small print.

•Stationery supplies, including:

    -Business-sized stationery and envelopes

    -Mailing envelopes of various sizes

    -Index cards

    -Sticky notes

    -Return address labels

    -File folders and labels

    -Printer paper and ink

•Stamps

•Tape

•Scissors

•Rubber bands

•Paperclips and binderclips

•Wastebasket/Recycling box

Chapter Four
A New Key

I've always said, today's mail is tomorrow's pile. Well what if you weren't getting as much mail? It seems like an easy solution to help clear off the piles of papers on the dining room table. But so many of us don't take the steps toward reducing the amount of paper in our homes. Some are afraid of letting go, thinking "What if I need it?" That's the same thinking they have for not throwing out a piece of paper they no longer use.

You want to end this vicious cycle, and you're encouraged by what you've read so far. But you're wondering where to begin.

Whether you want to go Almost Paperless™, or just get your papers organized, the solution is an effective file management system. But how do you develop one?

Who's Controlling Whom?
Let's first stop and think about how your mess got started.

A clean desk isn't important or necessary to everyone, but the ability to find information when you need it is. Perhaps you're afraid that if you neaten up, you'll forget what it is you need to do or never be able to find the papers again. If you have thousands of computer files, it could be very scary to go through and start sorting them.

Have you ever been late to an important engagement because you could not find the memo or evite and you had to spend 15 minutes looking for it? If so, then the paper (or evite buried in emails) is controlling you instead of the other way around.

When you have no file-management system or when the system you have isn't working, the unavoidable problems of paper in the 21st Century are compounded. You soon discover that you are writing notes about notes you have already written because you are afraid you won't find the first one. You want to use your cell phone to send you reminders, but you can't figure out how to do that. You have two calendars – one electronic and one paper, because when you're on the phone you make a few scribbles – but then forget to put it in your electronic calendar. You spend hours looking for that crucial piece of paper that you know you put someplace special but end up calling to get a duplicate because it is nowhere to be found.

The system described in the next chapters will assist you in deciding where your paper should go and help you accomplish the following objectives:
1. Eliminate unnecessary paper/files.
2. Avoid generating unnecessary paper.
3. Establish a location for essential paper/files.
4. Create a method for easy retrieval of paper/files.

Forget about the Backlog

When I first started as an organizing consultant and was faced with a huge backlog of client's papers, I thought that I should work with the client to eliminate that backlog first and then develop a system.

It didn't take long to realize that effective paper management means developing a system to stop feeling guilty over yesterday's pile and do something about today's. Instead of starting with the boxes that you never unpacked from your last move, last year's magazines that you never read, or even the unopened email messages from last month, start with today's mail!

A clean desk isn't important or necessary to everyone, but the ability to find information when you need it is.

Clutter is Postponed Decisions®

Have you ever looked at a pile of papers and said, "OK, today's the day. I'm going to clean up this mess." You pick up the first piece of paper—and think of any number of reasons why today isn't a good day to deal with it. You pick up the second and the third—and before you know it, the pile that was on the left side of the table is now on the right. You've just experienced one of the major principles of organization: Clutter is the result of postponed decisions. In the end, the only way to clear the clutter is to decide what to do with those pieces of paper or those documents cluttering your computer desktop.

Well, I've got good news for you! There are only three decisions you can make about any piece of paper or any computer file. To make it easier to remember, I call it the F–A–T system: File, Act, or Toss.

In my experience, every piece of paper in your life can be managed effectively by putting the piece of paper, or the information into what I call The Magic Six™:
    1. Desktop Trays
    2. Wastebasket/Recycle bin/Shredder
    3. Calendar
    4. Contact Management System
    5. Action Files
    6. Reference Files

Perhaps you're saying to yourself, "That's far too regimented for me. I could never do that."

The fact is you can. I've worked with dozens of clients who thought my system would never work, but they discovered they can adapt it to fit their particular style.

Here's how it works: File, act on or toss your papers. All the "act" or "file" papers you decide to keep fall into one of two categories—Action or Reference. Action papers are those you need to do something about. The tools you use for them are your calendar, your "To Do" list and your "Action Files." Reference papers contain information you want or need to keep for the future. The tools you use for those are your phone file/phone book and your "Reference Files."

Keep in mind the benefits of using the system. Imagine how it will feel to be able to clean off the kitchen counter when company is coming—and know that you will be able to find the credit card bill again tomorrow. Think of how much frustration—and embarrassment—you'll avoid when you're able to spend two minutes retrieving the directions to a business meeting instead of fifteen minutes trying to reach your client to get them again.

You will discover that not only is it possible to control the paper in your life, but the rewards greatly enhance the quality of your daily life as well.

Remember that today's mail is tomorrow's pile. Take today's mail to your paper-management center, and begin now to develop your own paper-management system.

Chapter Five

Computers and Paper

There are many books and blogs on the subject of personal computers and productivity. This is not the place for a major discussion about them, but these days they are a large part of managing your life and therefore your paper or documents. I will talk about ways to focus on using less paper throughout this book, and computers will not solve a paper-management problem by themselves.

Even if you go Almost Paperless™, you could instead end up with "stacks" of documents in your computer. You have not solved your problem – only moved it to a new location.

Even if you go Almost Paperless™, you could instead end up with "stacks" of documents in your computer.

You have not solved your problem – only moved it to a new location.

In fact, if a personal computer is used improperly, it can complicate paper management because it's so easy to create more paper. For example, you write a letter or a report and print out a copy to edit it. When you have completed the editing and entered the changes in the computer, you print out another copy. Within minutes you have doubled the amount of paper in your life.

Too Many Printouts

The computer will not make decisions for you. For example, people who use money management software often feel compelled to print out every report and document possible to ensure that they are getting the most out of their computer. What they often get is confused!

This is also a major reason that paper gets out of hand. The best approach is to print one of each report the first time or two you use a new program. Then study the reports and determine which ones are useful to you, and print only those. Keep in mind that any paper is of extremely limited value to you if you cannot identify specifically why you are keeping it. Ask yourself: "Under what circumstances would I use this information?" This not only cuts down on the amount of paper; it also cuts down on the amount of confusion.

Try storing reports electronically instead. You can save a lot of information on your computer and organize your files the same way you would if they were paper. You'll read more about that in later chapters. If you must print items, store them in your filing system whenever possible. For reports too large for the system, use binders to make the papers easier to manage and refer to. Label the binder as to contents and date. This will speed up the purging process considerably and will make the binders easier to access while they are still useful.

Make Your Computer Work for You

A computer can simplify many of your paper-management tasks. The computer is an excellent tool for maintaining a File Index. However, you may find it helpful to print out a copy to keep in front of your files. If you travel frequently and collect papers as you go, carrying your File Index—so you can put the key filing word on papers as you get them—will go a long way toward eliminating a paper pileup. Make entries and deletions by hand, and then periodically update it on the computer.

One of the most common uses of a computer in the home today is for financial management. The biggest advantage of using a computer instead of a manual system is that you will be forced to be consistent. It takes time to learn how to use the system, but many people have found it made a miraculous difference in their ability to manage their money.

Even if you decide not to use a complete money-management package, you can use your word-processing or spreadsheet program to keep track of numerous records.

For example, if you are frustrated by keeping track of membership and subscription records, you can list all of them in alphabetical order, with the date you renewed and for how long. The next time you get a bill for a magazine, pull up your list on the screen and you will know how long before the subscription actually expires. The same system works well for keeping track of charitable donations.

You can even organize your recipes. However, before you take that step, be sure the results will be worth the time and energy it will take to enter the data in your computer and to maintain it.

Computer Copy Versus Hard Copy

Many people believe that it must be preferable to keep documents in their computer rather than in their filing system. These days a 20-year-old might be able to pull up that document in just a few seconds with a keyword search. If you're using a web-based program such as PBWorks to store information, you will also be able to find things more quickly.

Although I advocate the use of less paper, when it comes to getting yourself organized, use whatever system works for you. For some of you, it might be easier to print "one-time documents" such as a thank you letter or a memo, and keep a copy in your reference files – but only if you might want to refer to it. (See Chapter 13.)

Preventing Disaster

The only thing separating a computer from a computer crash is time. You MUST back up your computer data. Many people feel more secure having a hard copy. But if your house goes up in flames, won't you lose all that paper you've so successfully managed? Many people use external hard drives to back up their files, but if your house catches fire, neither your computer nor that external hard drive will survive.

The best place to save a copy of all your data is in the Cloud, which refers to saving things on the Internet. Physically, this data will be stored in a server somewhere – probably in another state – but you will be able to access it from anywhere in the world with an Internet connection, no matter what happens to your computer.

So, if your house catches fire or a burglar steals your computer and external hard drive, you can go to your neighbor's house and use his/her computer to access your account for your homeowner's insurance.

Some backup storage services can cost as little as $5 per month. How much are you paying for that extra storage unit you use for extra office papers?

In addition, save early, save often. If your last backup was a year ago, you're still going to lose a lot of information. Depending on how often you use your files and computer, you should back up at least once a week so that your data is as up-to-date as possible. You can instruct the computer to conduct a backup each day or each week. You can also instruct it to do a modified backup—only those documents that have changed since the last time you backed up.

The most important thing is that, whatever you do, you do it consistently! How frequently will depend on how much you value your time and how critical the work is that you are doing.

Organizing Your Computer Documents

Have you ever sat in front of your computer scrolling up and down among the list of documents looking for the one you created a few months ago, last week—or even yesterday! And heaven forbid if someone else entered it and you are trying to find it!

You can use the same principles to organize documents in your computer as you do your hard-copy documents in your filing cabinet. For example, you may have folders for personal interests such as "Church," "Family" and "Journal," as well as folders for professional categories such as "Advertising," "Articles" (divided into subdirectories called "Education," "Medical," "Personal," etc.), "Fees," "Forms," "Overheads," "Outlines," "Procedures," "Promo," "Quotes," "Speeches," "Surveys" and "Video."

Although you can conduct a keyword search, for some, it might be easier to create an index of the folders and subfolders, just as I later describe in Chapter 13 for paper files, and keep a hard copy near the computer. Then, when you're working on a document and need to store it, you can refer to the index instead of roaming through the computer trying to determine where the document should go.

Computer Clean-Up

The same purging principles that apply to your paper files apply to your computer. Set up a regular schedule for cleaning out your computer files—even more frequently than you clean your paper files. In addition, each time I pull up a folder to add a new document, I do a quick check to see if there is an old one I can erase. Most of the time there is!

Children and Computers

Kids and computers go together. In fact, in many ways, they lead the way for fearful adults. Establish guidelines for your children's use of computers, and help them organize that resource.

If your children use your computer, create a separate folder in the computer for each child. If they create materials they wish to retrieve again, teach them to use folders to organize their documents.

Recycle Recycle Recycle

Recycle your used computer paper. Use the back for drafts. Cut it into various sizes to use as scratch paper beside your telephones and in the kitchen. If you prefer pads, you can take the paper to a commercial printer and have it cut and padded into handy pads for a small charge. (And, of course, there's always the bottom of the bird cage!)

People purchased more than 305 million new computers worldwide in 2009. Ninety-six million of those were in the U.S. Computer manufacturers expected another 366 million additional computers to be sold in 2010 – an increase of 20 percent. So what are people doing with the old machines? It is illegal to throw computers in the landfill, because of the harmful metals inside, including lead.

You can use your Zip code to find local recycling options for computers and other materials. Check out http://earth911.com/. For information on donating your computer to a charity or school, go to: http://www.computerswithcauses.org/.

Chapter Six
Paper or Electronic

In the rest of the book I'll talk about some organizing principles that will help you whether you prefer paper files or have (almost) everything stored on your computer.

For some of you, part of getting organized will be to make the shift from using paper to Almost Paperless™. Where do you begin?

First, why bother? If you're reading this, you probably already have some reasons for considering Almost Paperless.™

Did you know that every year enough paper is thrown away to make a 12-foot wall from New York to California? The amount of wood and paper we throw away is enough to heat 50 million homes for 20 years.

One study says that although 10,000 sheets of paper may only cost $30,000 at purchase, by the time you factor in photocopy, printing, faxing, mailing, courier and storage costs, you end up spending $447,000!

With statistics like those, it makes sense to cut back on the amount of paper we use. If you're not used to using computers for your life's business, then some of these might be difficult. Even just one small step can help you save trees and the cost of expensive printer ink! However, for some of you, it might be difficult to pay the necessary attention to bills if you can't physically touch them. If so, you can try just one or two of these easy steps toward reducing paper:

1. Start with your bills.
Mail is one of the main ways paper enters your home. Cutting back on how much mail is coming in will inevitably cut back on the paper you have to manage. Start with the main mail you receive: your bills. These days, postage and paper cost so much that many billers are offering incentives for going paperless. You might see it right on the envelope. They want to send you the bill by e-mail, or allow you to view it online

through their website. This is secure, and has the advantage of keeping all bills stored electronically on that site.

Worried about not having a copy for later referral? It's right there online. For added peace of mind, you can download the bill and save it to your computer files.

Electric, phone, credit card and other bills can all be sent to you this way, cutting back on the amount of snail mail you receive. You may have one or two billers that do not allow an electronic version to be sent. My car payment and water bill still arrive in paper each month, despite my repeated inquires about going paperless. That will change someday. We will talk more about the paying your bills in Chapter 13.

2. Your bank.
No matter what bank you use, they should allow you to pay your bills online with them – all in one place. Many people get frustrated having to sign on to several different web sites, remember all those passwords and sign up for their bank account to be charged each month. But with your bank, you can pay them all one online location. Most can even be set up to remind you when bills are due.

> a. Take the time to make sure each of your bills is entered into the system. This might require you to track down the paper copy of your bill for the account number or other information.

> b. Even if the bill does not allow electronic payment, you can still pay it online. The bank will simply issue its own check to that company on the appointed date.

> c. If you don't have one already, try using a debit card. You can save yourself the money spent on those little pieces of paper (and a lot of time) by swiping a debit card (or credit card) instead of writing a check. Some even have rewards points just like your credit card that can later be used to buy things.

> d. Don't forget to have your bank switch to electronic statements.

3. Other Mail
Bills aren't the only thing showing up. Every day a new torrent of paper enters our lives—newspapers, magazines, catalogs, bills, requests for donations, memos, reminders, invitations, school papers, personal correspondence, and probably the most frustrating of all, "junk mail." Now that we're also dealing with e-mail, the problem is even worse, because it's so easy to send. Funny jokes and other forwards, quick questions, attachments you don't need and spam can all end up in your personal e-mail inbox each day. We'll talk more in later chapters about how to deal with these items once they arrive, but what can you do to cut back on them before they arrive?

Paper or Electronic

Whenever you place an order from a catalog or request information about a product or a service online, you can be certain your name will be passed on to other companies. Even the telephone-directory companies sell mailing lists!

If you have difficulty throwing away "junk mail" or would prefer not to have to, you can explore ways to remove yourself from mailing lists. For snail mail, one of those resources is the Mail Preference Service (MPS), a consumer service sponsored by The Direct Marketing Association. You can access information by visiting their website at http://www.the-dma.org and clicking on consumer assistance. All instructions and forms are on the website.

Other ways you can reduce the amount of mail/email you get include:

• Many applications and order forms (both paper and online) contain a box you can check if you do not wish to be put on the other mailing lists. Check the box! Online, it might also say something like, "Yes! I'd like to receive information from Company X about deals and special offers." In that case, DO NOT check the box.

• Create a form letter/email and send it to all the organizations whose mailings you'd rather not receive at home or at the office and ask them to remove your name from their databases. At the very bottom of every email subscription newsletter is fine print that will allow you to unsubscribe. Click on it, and it usually generates an automatic email to the company.

• Be very careful about giving out your name, address, and phone number. If you do, request that your name be placed on an "in-house list" only. Lately I have noticed that local stores will ask for my phone number or email address when routinely ringing up an order. At first I just gave the information without thinking, but now I simply say that I would rather not give it out, and the reaction is always "Oh, OK." It is not necessary to know all this information simply so I can make a purchase; they are just building their mailing list.

• Avoid the Post Office's change of address system when moving. Unless you want the Post Office selling your name over and over again, send your own postcards.

• If you return warranty cards, add a note saying that you want your name kept private. You are covered by the manufacturer's warranty whether you return the card or not. The only reason to return a card is to find out about product recalls. Provide only your name, address and product serial number. If you check that you are interested in computers, you are sure to hear from computer companies!

• Don't enter any sweepstakes.

• Immediately delete any joke forwards from your random cousin or brother-in-law. This has the added benefit of preventing you from clicking on any links that may turn out to be viruses.

For even more ideas to stop unwanted mail, check out the Good Advice Press book, Stop Junk Mail Forever. (http://www.goodadvicepress.com/sjmf.htm)

Unfortunately, there is no guaranteed way to eliminate all you don't want, but the above steps will be a start. The overwhelming majority of papers you receive in the mail will eventually end up in the garbage anyway. The issue is whether or not they will first be allowed to collect dust in your home or collect virtual dust in your computer.

4. Your calendar.
In Chapter 9, we will talk in great detail about how keeping a good calendar will save you piles and piles of paper. But first, let's think about the calendar itself in paper form versus electronic. How are you keeping track of appointments, to-dos and family events? Maybe you have one master calendar in the kitchen, maybe you have a large leather-bound book you cart around. Each person's calendar needs are different; some people even keep more than one for work and personal. (However, I recommend keeping one calendar so that you never miss anything or forget an appointment on one that applies to the other.)

These days, you can buy a portable electronic calendar or use the one that comes with your smartphone. There are also many web-based calendars out there that can be accessed online through your phone and computer. These can be updated and changed with just a few clicks, whether you use an Android-based phone, a Blackberry or an iPhone.

Moving your calendar to an electronic format may be challenging for some. There's something really satisfying about filling in the little blanks on a piece of paper with your activities and events. That's OK. There are no hard and fast rules about the steps toward Almost Paperless™. Again, the bottom line is: what you decide to do is not as important as doing it consistently.

5. Resist the urge to print.
Many people (like me) prefer to print out e-mails to read them, or print out pdf documents for easier comprehension. I've observed that people in the 20-something age group do this far less than other age groups. Why? They are used to reading things on a monitor. One of the best things you can do to go Almost Paperless™ is to resist the urge to print pages. Stop and ask yourself, "Why am I printing this? Do I really need a hard copy? Can I try reading it on the monitor?" You might even consider a bigger monitor. I actually recommend two monitors for those going Almost

Paperless™, because it makes it easier to switch back and forth among different programs, e-mail and open Internet windows.

6. Consider a scanner.

Notice I said, "consider". Not everyone wants to take the time to scan in the papers they have now. If you want to start, just start with the new ones coming in. If you switch to paperless billing and ditch the junk mail, you'll have less paper at home anyway, and the few items you have can easily be organized into file folders. If you don't want to scan in items yourself, you can check out programs such as Shoeboxed (http://www.shoeboxed.com/), which will send you an envelope. You put your receipts and business cards in there, send it off, and they scan it for you.

7. Help Your Children Keep Their Paper Organized

As any parent knows, children are a huge source of paper in the home. We'll discuss this more in Chapter 20, but the first step is to teach your children about paper as they begin bringing it home from school.

A Note About Security

Many people are afraid that by keeping information online they won't be as secure. Identity thefts actually occur far more often from paper than from online hackers. Still, that's no reason to be careless. Just as you lock your car door, you should run adware and malware scans on your computer and use strong, unique passwords (at least eight characters, mix of numbers, letters and symbols). Avoid using your credit card on websites that don't appear legitimate. (Note: Look in the web address at the top. If it has https:// instead of just http://, it is a secure site for your credit/debit card.) Your bank and credit card companies will NEVER send you emails asking you to send updated information about your Social Security number or other private information.

Don't wait to take actions to prevent identity theft. You can be proactive in reducing your chances of becoming a victim by using some simple strategies.

• Never give out your Social Security number to anyone – unless the agency requesting it can guarantee confidentiality.

• Take your Social Security number off your driver's license and checks.

• Cancel and cut up unused or "extra" credit cards.

• Check your credit card statements for any purchases that seem odd to you – keep track of what you buy!

• Watch your phone bill, cable bill, internet bill, etc., for any increase in charges.

• If your credit card bill is late or you suspect it is lost, call the credit card issuer immediately.

• Check with your creditors on their policy for stolen cards or fraudulently accessed accounts. (You could be liable!)

• Mail bills from the post office or official postal box instead of your home.

• Keep important documents, (passport, birth certificate, stocks, savings accounts), locked in a safe deposit box or file drawer.

• Shred old bank and credit card statements, making sure account numbers, passwords, and addresses are unreadable before discarding.

• THINK about what you are throwing in the trash. Assume anyone can and will go through it after it leaves your home!

• Keep a written record or photocopy (locked away) of the contents of your wallet or purse. Don't carry your wallet with you when it is not necessary.

• Create passwords that make sense to you but are not the usual birth date, anniversary, pet or maiden name.

• Use only web sites that are encrypted and secure and have a privacy policy – before you type in your credit card number.

It is helpful to check your credit report annually as well. You should request this information from all three credit agencies (TransUnion (800) 888-4213; Experian (888) 397-3742; Equifax (800) 685-1111) and verify that the information they give you is correct. You can also go to https://www.annualcreditreport.com/cra/index.jsp to view your credit report. It's free. In addition, ask these agencies to put a "Fraud Alert" on your account, so that before anyone can borrow money they have to contact you in person.

Here's what to do if you think you may be a victim of this crime:
  -Contact the fraud department of all three credit agencies (listed above) and report your findings.
  -Call your financial institutions or creditors for any accounts that have been fraudulently accessed or opened and close these accounts.
  -Report the identity theft to the police. Get a copy of the police report to give to your creditors for poof of the crime.
  -File a complaint with the Federal Trade Commission 1-877-ID-THEFT, (http://www.ftc.gov/bcp/edu/microsites/idtheft/.)

Chapter Seven

Sort Short

Once Isn't Always Enough

Deciding where to begin is, for many people, the biggest paper-management stumbling block. One day you look at the top of the desk and decide that the situation has gone far enough. You're tired of looking at the piles of paper and spending hours sifting through them looking for important information. So you start with one pile, but before long, you come across some papers you don't feel like acting on or can't decide what to do with for one reason or another. You put down that pile and start with another. The same thing happens.

Before you know it, three hours have passed and the only thing that has changed is the clock, which said 9:00 when you began and now says 12:00. You feel even more discouraged!

For now, ignore all those old piles. The time will come to deal with them, and you will become more skilled at doing it as you practice.

Organizing Your Desktop

Earlier I mentioned the Magic Six™:

      1. Desktop Trays
      2. Wastebasket/Recyle Bin/Shredder
      3. Calendar
      4. Contact Management System
      5. Action Files
      6. Reference Files

Let's go through each of those and examie how they will help you manage your paper and files, starting with desktop trays.

Based on 30+ years of experience, I've found that MOST people benefit from three categories within reach of where they sit to manage paperwork:

1) To Sort – for papers/mail which require your decision

2) Out – for papers that need to go elsewhere – e.g., the mailbox, the office

3) File – for papers you need to file in another location

Begin by putting today's mail, or whatever pile of papers you wish to organize, into your "To Sort" tray. Don't feel that it has to be a tray. A box, bin, basket, shelf, or just a designated spot on a desk or table will do nicely.

If you're organizing your computer files, your computer desktop (screen) is a good place to create your "To Sort" tray. It's right in front of you – a visual reminder that you need to go through those items and make decisions.

Many people refer to the "To Sort" tray as their "In Box," but I shy away from the term. Often people are not clear about the meaning of "In," and I find mail weeks or even years old in the bottom of their "In Box" – especially in e-mail inboxes! Soon it becomes a hiding place for postponed decisions or undesirable tasks. One effective way of keeping papers visible is to use a vertical "in-box" so that the papers stand up and you can flip through them quickly.

The "To Sort" tray is a temporary spot for papers that you have not yet identified (sorted out), i.e., the mail you grabbed out of the box, papers given to you by other family members, papers picked up at a meeting or taken out of your own briefcase. In fact, you may need to have a "To Sort" tray on each floor to transport papers from purses, pockets, drawers, etc. to your desk for action.

"Well," you say, "there's nothing so special about that. I already have sixteen "To Sort" piles all around the house. There's even one in the bathroom! And I've got half a dozen on my desk at work. I'm very good at "To Sort" piles!" Here's where the discipline comes in. To make the "To Sort" tray work for you, you must learn to:

1. Sort short. Be prepared to keep your papers in this temporary resting spot only for a short time. Maybe you need to set a time limit for those papers, or set a specific time each day or week to go through them. Use whatever works for you, as long at it helps you find the willpower to attack those decisions regularly.

2. Use your "To Sort" spot consistently.

The trick to changing your habits and making this system work is to do the sorting frequently, before the next pile begins. Your "To Sort" tray is the place for papers to rest until you can get to the sorting. If it is becoming a permanent home, you are not sorting often enough.

You may have heard the expression, "Handle a piece of paper only once." For the majority of the people I know, this is impossible. I think it is possible and desirable, however, to handle a piece of paper only once more after it has been placed in the "To Sort" tray.

Remember, the "To Sort" tray is a temporary resting place. The paper should stay there just long enough for you to determine what you need to do with it next—File, Act, Toss. In some cases, it will go directly into the wastebasket (see Chapter 8), or you will want to take immediate action, so one handling will be enough. In many cases, you will move it from "To Sort" into another part of your paper-management system. The next several chapters describe in detail the five places your paper might belong in the system.

Chapter Eight

Master the Art of Wastebasketry®

With both electronic and paper documents surrounding us, it's easy to get overwhelmed. When you're ready to attack the contents of your "To Sort" tray, start by eliminating any paper or email that's easily identifiable as unnecessary. It is not accidental that the wastebasket comes at the top end of the Magic Six™ paper-management system; if you can learn to toss unneeded paper, emails or files as soon as you encounter them, you're on your way toward effective paper and file management.

My experience has shown that we never use roughly 80 percent of the items we collect! Years of dealing with people and their paper have convinced me that the ability to achieve goals is directly related to a willingness to use the wastebasket — or the delete button. There's no doubt that, in the long run, your stress level will decrease as the amount of paper or files in your wastebasket/recycle bin increases.

When I first began my career as a professional organizing consultant, I had nightmares that a distressed or irate client would call after I had helped them eliminate some of the paper in their life. In more than 30 years, it has never happened! There are very few pieces of paper or computer documents we can't live without, and most of us would improve the quality of our lives significantly if we eliminated a lot more.

"Do I Really Need This?"
Each day brings a world of opportunities—frequent-flyer bonus offers, entertainment and educational opportunities, information about new services and stores, magazines or blogs with articles you want to save (travel, hobbies, recipes, etc.). In order to take advantage of any of these opportunities, you need to be able to retrieve the appropriate information at the right moment.

Uncontrolled information is a burden, not a resource, and it is one that has only grown worse with the invention of the Internet. A pile of magazines with interesting, informative articles soon become dust collectors that take up space. Your RSS reader is full of feeds that have not been read, and you begin to feel guilty about all that information you have not yet absorbed.

Get tough. Take each piece of paper, electronic document, link or email and analyze it by asking each of the following questions. This may be difficult at first, but after a while you'll run through the questions automatically, and you will actually begin to enjoy throwing things out. When working with paper, I play a game with myself to see how many I can get in the wastebasket before they even make it to the desk!

Here are the questions to ask yourself:

1. Did I ask for this information?
Much of the information we receive is sent to us automatically because of computer mailing lists, or by friends and relatives who send us articles they think might interest us.

2. Is this the only place the information is available?
Is it in a book you already have? Can you find it online? (These days, that answer is most likely yes.) Would it be easy enough to get the information from the library or a colleague if you decided you really needed it? Do you have a CD or DVD with the same information? Is the information stored in your computer? As discussed in Chapter 6, one way to get rid of extra paper is take companies up on the offer of checking your balance online or to receive your statements via e-mail.

3. Would it be difficult to replace?
I am a member of several non-profit boards. Recently I looked at file after file of meeting minutes and decided that I did not need to keep these, since we have a board secretary whose job it is to keep records. If I ever needed to reference a file, all I have to do is access the board files.

4. Is the information recent enough to be useful?
A two-year-old restaurant directory is of limited value. A mailing list for a party given four years ago will be highly inaccurate.

5. Can I identify the specific circumstances when I would want this information?
"Just in case" is not a sufficient answer. If you cannot identify how you would use the information, it is unlikely that you would remember that you have it or be able to find it. Keep in mind Hemphill's Principle: "If you don't know you have it, or you can't find it, it is of no value to you."

6. Are there any tax or legal implications?

Would the IRS request this information in the event of an audit? Is there any possibility of a lawsuit related to this information?

If the answer to all the above questions is "No," but you're still reluctant to throw that piece of paper away, then ask this question:

7. What's the worst possible thing that could happen if I didn't have this piece of paper?
If you can live with the consequences, toss the item immediately!

Remember: Always open your mail next to the "circular file"—the wastebasket. And don't be afraid of your email's "delete button." Both will make it easier for you to toss things out, and throwing the paper on the floor beside you would only make extra work! Always ask yourself, "Do I really need or want to keep this?"

Years of dealing with people and their paper have convinced me that the ability to achieve goals is directly related to a willingness to use the wastebasket – or the delete button.

In the first few months of my career as an organizing consultant, I was hired by a highly respected professional to organize her condominium. When I opened her door, I was shocked to see piles of paper, several feet deep, surrounded by small piles of paper that were obviously multiple attempts to "get organized." She confessed that she had finally called me after the condominium association sent someone to do a routine spraying for insects and he reported that her home had been ransacked! Since that incident, I have met dozens of people who have not had guests in their homes for years because they were too embarrassed by their piles of paper. Don't let that happen to you.

Recycling
I often refer to the wastebasket as part of the File-Act-Toss system. But if you're throwing away lots of paper, consider putting it into a recycling bin. Each ton (2,000 pounds) of recycled paper can save 17 trees. And paper production accounts for 35 percent of the trees we cut down.

There are a variety of recycling opportunities. Check with your city or county government for bins that they can pick up from your house along with your garbage. You can also donate newspapers, magazines and boxes to organizations or individuals that will put them to good use. You can use your Zip code to find local recycling options for computers, batteries, cell phones and other items that contain materials you cannot throw into landfills. Check out http://www.1800cleanup.org.

One client of mine had stacks of beautiful art-related magazines in her office. She admitted that she never read them but could not bear to part with them—until we found a group shipping magazines to libraries in Poland. It was quite a sight to see, her red Jaguar stuffed with magazines with just enough room for the driver!

The Issue of Privacy
For some people, one of the stumbling blocks to getting rid of paper is the issue of privacy. Unfortunately, identity theft and other information thefts are becoming a bigger issue.

If your personal information is on the paper, it's probably better to shred it. As I mentioned earlier, the Better Business Bureau says identity theft is more prevalent offline with paper than it is with our online accounts. Personal shredders are inexpensive and sold readily at office stores, Target and Wal-Mart. The results of your personal destruction can even be recycled for packing material, cat litter or confetti.

Chapter Nine

Your Calendar

The purpose of many of those pieces of paper and emails/files you collect is to remind you to do something. As a result, you can eliminate a considerable amount of paper from your desks, dresser tops, mirrors, purses and wallets simply by effectively using an important tool in our Magic Six™: your calendar. The key here is to get into the habit of extrapolating the information you need from the paper/file, entering it on your calendar, and then throwing out the pieces of paper or — if you really think you'll need the information in the future — filing it in Reference.

The most productive people I know have a "master calendar" on which all commitments—business and personal for all family members—are recorded.

Calendars used in the way I'll describe in this chapter not only help eliminate paper and file clutter, but also the mind clutter that comes from having to remember too many details and dates at one time.

Your "Master Calendar"
Once upon a time, keeping track of our schedules was fairly simple. Husbands went off to work and kept their business schedules at the office. If an after-work business appointment needed to be made, the husband—ideally—called home first to be sure there was no conflict. Wives kept the home running smoothly, keeping track of the kids' schedules and making sure social engagements weren't missed.

Life is not so simple anymore. Now mom and dad are both working and juggling Johnny's swimming lessons and Susie's soccer practice along with their work appointments and social engagements.

The most productive people I know have a "master calendar" on which all commitments—business and personal for all family members—are recorded. If you're fortunate enough that you can keep your business life separate from your personal life, you can keep one calendar at the office and another at home. But if you're like most people, you'll need the combined business/personal "master calendar," which you might keep at home or in the office—or perhaps it will be a portable one that you carry with you in a briefcase, your suit-jacket pocket or purse.

You may ask, "How important is it to carry my calendar with me?" These days, just about everyone needs to carry a calendar. If you do not already carry a calendar with you, one way to determine whether it would be helpful for you is to keep track for several days of how many times you would have referred to your calendar if you had it with you.

Coordinating Your Schedule

A major complication of calendars is coordination. Keeping associates and family members informed of changing commitments is an ongoing challenge.

If you need to coordinate calendars with someone at work, develop a consistent system appropriate for your circumstances. For example, if you make some appointments and your assistant makes others for you, agree on when and how you will communicate changes. One possibility is for your assistant to check your calendar each morning. A client of mine pastes a few one-inch removable notes in the back of his calendar and uses them to note appointments he makes. Then he sticks them on his assistant's desk as he goes by.

Most families find it crucial to hang a calendar in some strategic location in their house to communicate information that affects the family, such as travel and sports schedules, family celebrations or doctors' appointments. Many people put their calendar on the refrigerator, since everyone ends up there sooner or later!

We talked a little bit in Chapter 6 about electronic calendars. Since many people are keeping electronic calendars, it might be useful to find one that enables you to share your calendars.

> *For example, with web-based calendars such as iCal and Gmail's calendar, you can "share" your calendar with someone else so they can see your activities. These can be color-coded per person, and if necessary, marked "private" so certain activities are not specified, but are noted on the calendar.*

I know one couple who does this effectively using Gmail's calendar. They even add in other event calendars, such as the theater, which is available online, so that those events appear automatically.

It won't be long before family calendars are kept on the family iPad or other tablet, but if you're not there yet, you probably want to keep a paper master calendar on the refrigerator.

Put Your Calendar to Work

Here's how it works. Let's say you receive a neighborhood meeting notice in the mail. Frequently you can enter the information—time, place, telephone number—directly into your calendar and throw the notice away. Once you start receiving these types of communications via email, the same principle still applies: Enter the information into your electronic calendar and then delete the evite or excess message.

If there is more essential information on the notice than will fit in your calendar, such as an agenda, directions, etc., you can note the name of the meeting in your calendar and put the notice itself into "Pending" (see Chapter 11). Put a "P" beside the notation in your calendar, so you will know that further information can be found in your "Pending" file.

Suppose you read in the newspaper about a concert you would like to attend, if you can get home from work in time and if there are no other family obligations. Put the date of the concert in your calendar—in pencil—both on the day by which you must buy tickets and on the day of the event. If you simply leave the notice on your desk so that you won't forget, you are likely to handle that piece of paper dozens of times and still not attend the concert. Again, the same principle applies when electronic: You read the article online, click over to your iCal, and enter in the information. One minute later, you're back to your reading.

If you've emailed someone and you need to get a reply in two days, make a note to yourself in your calendar, "Heard from John?"

You can see that you can use your calendar not only as an appointment-keeper but as a tool for effective follow-up. If there are specific materials you want to remember to check when you follow up, make a note of that directly in your calendar. Some electronic calendars also have a specific area for "tasks" that can be scheduled on specific days or just remain off to the side in a list. There is even a little box you can click when the task is complete and it will cross the item out for you.

Make an Appointment with Yourself

In my experience, the people who are most successful in managing their time and accomplishing their goals are those who make appointments with themselves. I've found the most effective way to organize my life is to sit down every Sunday evening and identify the most important things I want to accomplish in the week ahead and note them in my calendar. Whenever you choose to do it, do it regularly. And when you do, determine the specific tasks you want to accomplish in various areas of your life. For example, if you are trying to improve your exercise habits, decide what days of the week you will exercise, and where and how you will do it.

You can also use your calendar to make notes to remind yourself to check on specific issues. For example, you're at a meeting and you agree to complete a certain task. Make a quick calculation about when you need to begin work and write a note to yourself on your calendar. If you don't, put an asterisk beside your note to remind you to enter the information in your calendar when you return home or to the office. In this way you avoid creating additional pieces of paper and you will be reminded at exactly the right time.

If there is a specific task you need to do for yourself (for example, clean out your file drawer or spend some time on your "To Read" pile—see Chapter 17), make an appointment with yourself, just as you would with someone else.

Some people hesitate to use this approach because they don't want to become too compulsive. They shudder to think of themselves talking to a friend and having to say, "I need to go now. I have to catch up on my reading!" I'm not suggesting such inflexibility!

Using your calendar as a time-management tool helps you to be realistic about your time. If you have blocked out an hour to write the minutes from your last committee meeting and you decide you would rather do something else or you have to take your child to the doctor, you can realistically decide on your options for that given day. You can write the minutes on your laptop while you are waiting at the doctor's office or block out time later in the week. Whatever you do, make sure you keep your commitment to yourself in one way or another!

Choose Your Calendar Wisely
I mentioned earlier that electronic calendars are another way to rid yourself of more paper. Electronic calendars have the benefit of going anywhere with you and being changed without erasing or crossing out old notes. They can even send you pop-up reminders to your phone or emailed reminders to your email inbox. There's an unlimited amount of space, and you can view your calendar by year, month, week or day. But if a paper calendar works better for you – even as you move your bills and your daily newspaper online – then continue to use it.

If you use paper, there are hundreds of calendars on the market and choosing one can be frustrating. Why? Well, many calendars are so complicated that you have to take a training course to learn how to use them. Keep in mind that just because a company includes something in a calendar or planner doesn't mean you have to use it!

You should consider a few things when you select your calendar. If you use your calendar as I've described, you need to select one with plenty of writing space. Of course, this will mean a larger calendar. If you don't regularly carry a purse or a briefcase, you may feel this is not practical and you will have to make adjustments. One alternative to give you additional writing space is to use the removable notes, which can be affixed to your calendar and removed when you have completed the tasks.

Format is the second factor to consider. Do you need to see each day, the month, the whole year, or a combination?

My experience is that the best paper managers use a combination—a weekly calendar for short-term planning, and a monthly or yearly one for long-term planning, and for recording "non-negotiable" appointments and reminders, such as travel schedule and children's birthdays. Franklin Covey makes some great calendars in different varieties.

I don't think I've ever met anyone who has found the "perfect" calendar. I hear comments such as, "This calendar is great, except it's too big," or "There isn't enough writing space." With your calendar, as with many things in life, you can have anything you want, but not everything you want. Many of my clients combine the best parts of two calendars.

Use Only What You Need

I once sat next to a woman on an airplane who was holding a beautiful leather-bound calendar with her name inscribed in gold. She suddenly let out a big sigh. "Is something wrong?" I asked. "I must be hopeless," she said. "My husband bought me this beautiful calendar, and I don't even know what to do with it!" We spent the next hour assessing her needs—and eliminated half of the pages in the calendar.

One of the best calendar options out there is the Planner Pad®. Clients of mine who hate all other calendars seem to like this one. I used their 81/2" x 11" version for 12 years. (I'm now electronic.) There's a two-page yearly calendar in the front with room for long-range planning and provides just enough space to write key words such as a client's name, the city where you'll be, your son's birthday, etc.

The rest of the Planner Pad® is made up of a series of two facing pages for each week. The pages are divided into three sections. The bottom third is for specific appointments Monday through Sunday from 7:00 a.m.—9:00 p.m. (I like the long hours, since I can easily include breakfast and dinner appointments.) The middle third I use for my daily "to do" lists—phone calls, reminders, etc.

The top third is what I used on Sunday evenings to identify my priorities for the week in each of the areas of my life. Also, there's room at the bottom of the right-hand page to note deductible expenses. This format is particularly pleasing when Uncle Sam calls! To increase usability, I purchased stick-on tabs to identify specific months of the year, and peel-off pockets for the front and back covers to hold receipts, business cards, etc. I cut off the corner of the page at the end of the week. The back of the Planner Pad® has pages that are great for "to do" lists. Learn more about Planner Pads at http://www.plannerpads.com.

Symbols for your Calendar

The following are some abbreviations I use on my calendar to help remind me of what I'm to do. As you think of others that you could use, add them to the list!

    C=Call

    CE=Calls Expected (they will call me)

    D=See "Discuss" Action File

    P=See "Pending" Action File

    LM=Left message

    NA=No answer

Chapter Ten
Your "To Do" Lists

Does this sound familiar? You're trying to go to sleep and you suddenly remember, "Oh, I never called my insurance company to take John off the automobile policy!" Or, while driving home from the hardware store, you realize you forgot to get that extra house key the cleaning service has needed for the past month.

Experiences like these are the basis for the piles of notes scratched on the back of empty envelopes, on the corner of the newspaper or on any scrap of paper that happens to be lying around. Many of the pieces of paper in the piles around the house and scattered over our desks at work are there to serve as reminders of things we want to do at some point in the future—tomorrow, next week, or maybe not until we retire!

One of the biggest problems with going Almost Paperless™ is resisting the urge to make little handwritten notes to ourselves. Even those with smartphones and laptops will still sometimes pull out a pen and a scrap of paper to make a note. If you want to avoid these scraps of paper, the trick is to find a place in your electronic life to put these notes and reminders.

To Do or Not To Do
First, let's look at the "To Do" list itself. It's another "Action" file (see Chapter 11), really, to provide a consistent place to compile notes to yourself, and in so doing to eliminate many pieces of paper from your life. Dorothy Sarnoff, chairman of Speech Dynamics, Inc., calls such a list "a depository for your thoughts."

Some people decry the whole idea, feeling that if they write something down they might absolve themselves from doing it! In fact, making a list of the things you need to do is the first step to developing a goal-setting technique that is essential for effective life management.

One of the major joys of a "To Do" list is crossing items off when they are completed. I put a check by the items I have completed on the daily "To Do" list. I always check the list from the two previous days. If I didn't get it done in three days, I try to figure out why, and what I can do about it. One client admitted that periodically he makes lists of things he's already done just so he can cross them off! In fact, I have discovered that if you spend a day dealing with crisis after crisis, and nothing on your "To Do" list gets checked off, it can be an excellent learning process to make a list of what you actually did. Then you can analyze the list to see if there was something you could have done to prevent the crisis.

What To Do First

Making a list of the things you need to do is the first step to developing a goal-setting technique that is essential for effective life management.

Success in life can come from doing things right—but first we have to make sure we are doing the right things. One of the ongoing issues for everyone I know—and for me as well—is deciding what to do first.

How do you decide? Let me suggest an exercise to assist you in improving your ability to decide what to do first.

Take a look at your life during the last several months. What results have you had during this time period that you would like to repeat? When I completed the exercise, I recognized that one of my most fulfilling activities was speaking to large audiences. When I analyzed how I got those opportunities, I could identify actions I needed to take to ensure that I could multiply my opportunities—namely, spending time developing relationships with meeting planners who have the ability to hire speakers for large audiences.

Or, to put it another way, what's one thing you could do that would bring about something you really want? When I asked myself that question, my answer was, "I want to be physically fit." My challenge then was identifying what specific actions I needed to take to make that happen.

How To Do It

There are probably as many kinds of "To Do" lists as there are list makers. Keep in mind that some "To Dos" are tasks that need to be done at a specific time such as mail a birthday card to Aunt Sally, while others are things you want to do but have not yet determined when you can do them, such as "buy birthday cards." Chances of completing the "To Dos" with specific dates improve if you enter them in your calendar (see Chapter 9). The rest of the "To Dos" go on a master "To Do" list, which may or may not be in your calendar.

People have different criteria for what they include in their list and how they include it. Some just use key words like "Call Jerry," but what if you look at the list and you can't remember why? Others add notes about the topic to be discussed and the phone number so they don't have to look it up when it's time to call. There is also the ongoing debate on whether to separate at-home to-dos from work to-dos. Some people keep a running list, and when it gets messy or full they start over.

The more information you want to put in your "To Do" list, the more cluttered your list will become, and the less helpful it will be. One solution for this is to devise coded symbols to record progress on a task. You can use many of the same ones you use on your calendar.

There are numerous software programs, web programs and electronic gadgets for managing "To Do" lists along with your calendar. Outlook, iCal and Gmail's calendar all come with "To Do" lists. You can assign the task a date or leave it alone, and some have a nice little box to check when you have completed the task. You can also create different "To Do" lists based on the categories described below or your own. If you are mostly paperless, you might try Evernote or other similar web-based programs for more broad notes to yourself. You can also use a Word document, a "sticky" on your computer desktop or some other system. I like web-based programs because they can later be accessed via smartphone – not just on my laptop.

Keeping your "To Do" list with your calendar is perfect for some people and completely frustrates others. The decision about how to do your "To Do" list will depend on how and when you use it. You may, in fact, have more than one list!

"Like with Like"

One basic principle when organizing anything is to "put like items together." Some people apply this principle to organizing lists.

> *Put items on a "To Do" list together based on the kind of activity required. For example, group together all phone calls, all letters to write and all errands to run. When you're running errands, you won't be distracted by a list of phone calls you need to make. Or if you are trying to make a series of phone calls, you won't be bothered by a note to buy batteries.*

Some people just keep a running list. I keep some "To Do" categories in the calendar I carry with me, such as "Errands" and "Numbers," while other categories stay in the loose-leaf book at home and in another book at the office. You can use temporary labels, notations in your calendar, or index cards in your pocket to remind yourself to enter a "To Do" on a list that is not accessible at the time.

By the way, one index card is cheaper than one sticky note and perfect for writing down ideas. Just be sure to put only one idea or item on each card.

You should also consider frequency of use when you decide where to list your "To Dos." Let me explain. One time I was discussing the subject of getting organized with a gentleman sitting next to me on an airplane. He commented, "Some of the things on my "To Do" list have been there for years." By the tone of his voice it was evident that he expected my disapproval—which he didn't get! There are certainly things I want to do that I've been thinking about for years—such as take a trip to Alaska and write a family history. I have an "Annual To Do List"—ideas for major projects that I consider once a year. (I keep that list in my computer. There's no point carrying it around with me.) So if you decide to have more than one "To Do" list, consider keeping them where you will most likely use them.

To Carry or Not to Carry?
Should you carry your "To Do" list with you? The proponents of the "To Do" list on a yellow legal pad might find this difficult. Some people use a small spiral notebook or even index cards they can stick in their pocket. Adhesive notes make a handy "To Do" list when you need to put a reminder in a "can't miss it" place—such as in the car, on the outside of your briefcase or purse or on the bathroom mirror.

A portable "To Do" list can be a big time saver. For example, if I'm near a shopping center and I have an extra ten minutes before I need to get to an appointment, I can check the "Errands" section in my list and find one or two things I can accomplish in that time.

Much To Do About Something
Your "To Do" list can be divided into lots of categories, depending on your specific needs. The following are some possibilities. If you think of others not described here, use the space in the margin to write them down. Keep in mind that you are the one who needs to determine not only the categories of your "To Do" list, but where it should be located physically.

If you are electronic, the same principles still apply – just add the categories to your computer or Smartphone list or calendar. Here are some suggestions:

Birthdays
Most of us have good intentions about remembering those special days of family members and friends. You can create a special section in your "To Do" book. This

makes it easy to translate onto your calendar the days you need to mail the cards or to purchase the cards you need when you are running errands. My personal solution for never forgetting a birthday has been Send Out Cards. You can try it out for yourself by going to http://www.sendoutcards.com/papertigerlady.

Books and Music

A lot of my clients keep torn, yellowed newspaper articles about books they have been meaning to purchase. The electronically savvy may have multiple links to articles about books. Instead, make a list of books you want to borrow from the library or buy. You can also list CDs or songs to buy or keep track of items you have loaned to friends.

Discuss

This category provides a place to accumulate information you wish to discuss with a particular person. Use one section for each person in your life with whom you interact frequently: boss, assistant, child, spouse, committee chair, etc. Use another to list questions you want to ask your doctor at your next appointment, another for mechanic questions, or another to list concerns you want to raise at the next parent-teacher conference at school.

Errands

Have you ever gone past the appliance repair shop wishing you had the style number of the vacuum bags so you could pick them up on the way home instead of making an extra trip? This category will save you many miles of errand running. (Check out our "To Do" Book, which has a pocket to put such receipts, dry cleaning receipts, etc. You can find it under "products" at barbarahemphill.com.)

Group errands together according to geographical area or type of store. Most people keep their grocery list in the kitchen, but if you happen to be at work when you think of something that needs to go on the list, this is a great place to put it. Then, when you are ready to go grocery shopping, you can combine both lists.

Gifts

Remember that "perfect gift" you found hidden in a closet after you spent two hours looking for a housewarming gift for your new neighbor? Here's a place to list the gifts you have on hand—and where they are located if you are afraid you will forget (Be careful, of course, about spoiling a surprise by listing gifts for the family). You can also make a note when you overhear your father saying he really would like to have a good pair of binoculars. You might even make a list of gift ideas for yourself, in case your kids ever ask! (I post mine prominently on the refrigerator just before Christmas and my birthday!) If you're looking for an electronic gift list, Amazon allows you to create a public "wish list" so that others can look you up and see what you want.

Goals
Research shows that fewer than three percent of the U.S. population put their goals in writing. It also shows that having written goals is high on the priority list of high achievers. Whether you are making New Year's resolutions or designing a business plan, this section provides a convenient place to keep track of your goals and your progress. Then it will be easy to check periodically to see if your life activities reflect what you said you wanted to do! (This qualifies as one of those categories you don't need to carry with you all the time.)

Letters/Emails
We all mean to write more letters/emails/Facebook messages than we ever do. Write one message a week, and you've kept in touch with 52 people. This section also could be divided into personal and business. If you enjoy writing real letters, do whatever you can to make it easy to keep in touch—take advantage of hotel stationery, buy postcards when you travel, or carry stationery with you. Otherwise, consider a smartphone that offers access to your email and social networking accounts. You can write some messages while you wait in line at the grocery store.

Numbers
Frequently the papers in our piles contain numbers we need to remember. Be cautious about listing numbers you don't want other people to know, such as pin numbers or passwords. However, having quick access to insurance policy numbers, club membership or frequent traveler numbers, as well as refill numbers or clothing sizes can be helpful. Cloud computing solutions provide great comfort for families scattered around the world and needing to share important information.

Phone Calls
List the names of people you wish to call, with the phone number beside them to speed up the process. You may find it helpful to use one section for personal calls and another for business. If you need to make a phone call at a specific time, use your calendar, rather than your "To Do" list (or use both—as a security measure).

Projects
Planning to redecorate your living room or give a Super Bowl party? Here is a place to collect all the ideas you have. (One client puts a small sample of her wallpaper, paint, fabric swatches etc. in her "To Do" book.) Then as you begin the project, you can enter the various steps into your calendar as they need to be completed.

Restaurants
Here you can record names of restaurants you would like to try, with addresses and phone numbers and business hours. Group the restaurants together by geographical area. Then, if you are meeting a friend or client downtown, you can easily check your list to see which restaurant would be most suitable and convenient.

This system will help to eliminate all the pieces of paper with restaurant reviews you have been saving, and it's also fun when a guest comes to town and says, "Let's go out tonight." It will take you no time at all to choose your restaurant.

Thoughts

How many times have you read a quote that intrigued you or had a brainstorm about how to solve a particular problem and said to yourself, "I'll have to give that some thought"? Write those ideas down. If you carry them with you, and find yourself caught in rush hour traffic, or waiting in the doctor's office with nothing to do, you can decide what step you need to take next!

Travel

A "To Do" book is a terrific place to put a standard packing list for travel. Then each time you plan a trip to a new city, create a special page. Make notes about particular things you want to take with you, people you want to see or places you want to go, or information about car rentals, hotel reservations, etc. Finally, make a "Before Trip Checklist" to remind you about those last-minute "To Dos," such as checking the thermostat, turning off the coffee pot, making arrangements to feed the cat, and stopping the mail. Some frequent travelers make an "After Trip Checklist" to remind themselves of things they may want to do differently on the next trip.

Remember I said that one of the objectives of this paper-management system is to eliminate unnecessary pieces of paper. Try just these first aspects of the system—the desktop trays, the wastebasket, the calendar, and the "To Do" list—and see how many you can toss. For those pieces of paper you have to keep, remember you can divide them into two categories: Action or Reference.

Caution!
Clean out your "To Do" list from time to time. If lists become overwhelming, ask yourself these questions:

- *Is there someone who could help me get this done?*
- *Is there a way to simplify this task?*
- *Would it matter if I put it off for _____ days / weeks / months?*
- *What's the worst possible thing that could happen if I didn't do this?*

Chapter Eleven

Your Action Files

After you have eliminated as many pieces of paper as possible by using your recycle bin/shredder, your calendar and your "To Do" list, the remaining papers will fall into one of two categories:

Action files - Action files are for those papers that need your attention immediately or at some point in the near future (as opposed to the "some day" projects).

Reference files - Reference files are for information you know you will, or think you might, need at some point in the future. Some of this information can be "filed" in your phone book; suggestions for doing so are in the next chapter. Chapter 13 also covers ways to create an effective Reference file.

Taken together, the system is particularly effective if you keep two points in mind:

1. A Reference File can become an Action File or vice versa.

For example, a reference file called "Entertaining" can become an action file if you are planning a party. When the party is over, look through the contents of the file, discard material you won't need again, and return the remaining material to your reference files (This is an important step that many people omit!). Be sure to take a few minutes to throw out any excess papers at this point, instead of saying, "I've got to clean that file out someday." It is much quicker and easier to do while the information is fresh in your mind.

2. You can have an Action File and a Reference File with the same or similar file headings.

For example, you might have a reference file entitled "Community Association" for papers you need to keep but which don't require action, and an action file entitled "Community Association—Dues Campaign" for a current project.

Keeping action files on the computer is similar. For some, it will be easiest to create two main folders called "Action" and "Reference" and create sub-folders within those to further organize items. For others, it may be easier to create topic folders for each item and create sub-folders within those for reference and action items. It depends on how many items you have, the way your brain will think to look for the items you need, and how you want to search for documents.

To determine the permanent action categories into which a particular piece of paper falls, ask yourself, "What is the next action I need to take on this piece of paper?"

When Action Is Too Packed

Clients with great piles of paper on their desks will frequently say, "I need all of this on my desk because I am working on it." But often a close look will determine that even though all the papers on the desk might need to be saved (although that's not always true, either!), not all of them are necessary to complete the particular project. A bulky action file often indicates that some of those papers could go in a reference file, or you may need two or more action files for one project, such as "Party—Menus" and "Party—Invitations."

If you lead a very simple or Almost Paperless™ lifestyle, you may find that one file called "Action" is all you need, but for many people a pile of papers that need action would soon topple over. When the pile gets that deep, it is difficult to do anything. It soon takes as much time to find a project as it does to complete it.

Because computer files aren't creating a visual pile on your desk, it can be tempting to create more and more files and documents without pausing once in awhile to clean out the old. All you need is a keyword to search and presto! —you can find it. It will be quite awhile before you run out of space.

But think about this: One of my clients had more than 7,000 emails before she began to run out of storage space. Someday, those limits might not even be there, but it took her a lot more time to go through the old ones than if she had deleted a few more along the way.

The Next Step

Remember that clutter represents postponed decisions. To simplify the decision-making process, it is helpful to recognize that the papers we need to take action on fall into two basic categories. I call them "Temporary Actions" and "Permanent Actions." Temporary Actions are things you are going to do that will come to an end: a trip you will be taking, a party you are planning, a purchase you're going to make.

Permanent Actions are those you do over and over again, such as making phone calls, paying bills or writing letters.

To determine the permanent action categories into which a particular piece of paper falls, ask yourself, "What is the next action I need to take on this piece of paper?" It is crucial that you recognize the significance of the word "next" in this question, as the answer will tell you into which action file to put the paper. There are several possible answers to the question, and each answer is an action file category.

Sometimes it takes time to find the answer. For example, you have received a letter from Joe with a question about changing the membership qualifications for an association to which you belong. Your initial reaction may be, "I have to call Joe," but you realize you need to speak with Nancy first to get her opinion, and you can't talk intelligently to her until you've read the association's bylaws.

Joe's letter requires three actions: read the bylaws; call Nancy; and call Joe. You would therefore first put the letter in your "Call" action file with a temporary note on it to "Call Nancy" and "Call Joe." Then make an appointment with yourself (noted in your calendar) to "Read bylaws." Add C-Nancy/C-Joe" to the note as a reminder that you're reading the bylaws to get information you can discuss in a call with Nancy before you call Joe.

Potential Action File Categories

Here are descriptions of a number of categories for action. Don't be intimidated by the number of categories — you probably won't need them all — and you might decide you need others that aren't included here. If, as you read the list, the whole idea begins to seem overwhelming, choose a few categories that have particular appeal to you and try them. If you're anything like the thousands of people who have already adopted the system, you'll soon love it and wonder how you ever managed without it.

If you are Almost Paperless™, your files for these may be documents saved on your desktop, or a label or folder for the emails in your inbox. The point is not specifically how you practice these principles, but that they still can be applied in the Information Age.

Call

Many times the next action required on a piece of paper is a telephone call to someone. In addition to putting the paper in the "Call" file, you may also wish to make a note on your calendar on the day you need to make the call. Using a symbol such as "C" will remind you that there is additional information in the "Call" file.

Calls Expected

You receive a telephone call in which the conversation begins, "Hello. This is Anne Smith. I am returning your call." A knot forms in your stomach as you frantically try to remember why you called her—or even who she is! If you have a note in your "Calls Expected" file that tells you why you have left a message for that person to return your call, it can be a real stress-saver.

In addition, you can review the file periodically to check the current status of the calls. Were you simply returning her call, and the ball is now in her court, or do you really want to talk to her? If the former is the case, after a period of time you can throw the paper out. If it's the latter, take the paper out of "Calls Expected" and put it in "Call," with a note on your calendar to make the call again.

Computer/Smartphone Entry

Some of the papers on your desk contain information that needs to be entered into your computer (or now, your smartphone). It will be more efficient to make several entries at the same time—or delegate it to someone else to enter. When you've entered the material from this file into the computer, either throw out the papers, pass them on to someone else who may need them, or, if you must save them, move them to the appropriate reference file.

Why, you may ask, if I'm helping you organize your paper, would I suggest you keep paper after you've entered the information in your computer? The simple answer is that there are instances when you need to keep the paper. For example, you might track your investments on a computer, but you still need records of transactions for tax purposes. Be very careful what you do keep; it's all too easy to enter information and keep the paper anyway, "just in case." Ask yourself, "What's the worst thing that could happen if I don't have this paper?" Can you live with the consequence? If so, toss; if not, file.

Discuss

Communication is a key to managing the paper in our lives. Frequently we can't act on a matter until we have discussed it with another person. All of us have certain people in our lives with whom we routinely discuss issues, whether it is a spouse, a child, a colleague, a friend, or a professional resource. The "Discuss" category can contain several subcategories. For example, "Discuss—Mary," "Discuss—Accountant." If you need to discuss a particular piece of paper by a specific time, put a reminder in your calendar.

File

Of course, it's easiest to file immediately. But people dislike filing and will put it off as long as possible. Even if you don't mind filing, the filing cabinet may be in another room. Either way, you will need a "File" for those pieces of paper that need to go into the reference files. Many of the pieces of paper that arrive in the mail can go directly into "File" and never clutter the top of your desk. If your documents are already electronic, I urge you to try filing them as they come in. It's as easy as a few mouse clicks and then the item is done. We'll talk about filing more in Chapter 13.

Pay

This is the category to put all the bills you need to pay, as well as any other paper that requires writing a check, an order you wish to place or a donation you would like to make. If your household finances are quite complicated, you may wish to subdivide this category. For example, you could have a "Must Pay" for mortgage, utilities and car payment and a "Would Like to Pay" for potential donations, orders, subscriptions. If you pay some of the bills and your spouse pays others, you may wish to subdivide the category into "Pay—Betty" and "Pay—Bob." This is also a good place to put reminders of deductions that are automatically taken from your checking account.

Pending

Many names have been applied to this category: "suspension," "tickler" or "bring up." This is not a place to put papers that require action from you at this time. Rather, it is for papers that will require action at some future date, or that will require action after you have received additional information.

When you're tempted to put a piece of paper in this category because you're uncertain of your decision, ask yourself, "What am I going to know tomorrow that I don't know today?" If the answer is "Nothing," you will know that you need to look further into the issue to find out what other category the paper really belongs in.

If you simply cannot make a decision at this time and you want to postpone the decision, put the paper in "Pending," but make a note on your calendar to remind you to consider the issue again. If you receive a dinner invitation and with the invitation are directions for getting to the host's home, put the invitation in "Pending" with a symbol such as "P" beside the engagement notation on your calendar. If, however, you check your "Pending" file each day, it isn't necessary to put the cross-referenced note in your calendar.

If you have many "Pending" items, you may want to create a 1-31 file—one for each day of the month—and put the piece of paper in the file for the day you'll need it. A wonderful example of this is called SwiftFile. You can learn more about the SwiftFile Solution at http://www.barbarahemphill.com/swiftfile-solution.

Photocopy

Often you can't take the next action on a piece of paper until you make a photocopy, as in the case of submitting medical insurance claims. As medical records become electronic, that may change. These days there are fewer items that need to be photocopied. Remember, tackling your paper problem means thinking about each piece of paper you create. In the past, you might have wanted to photocopy an article from the newspaper to send to your sister and keep the original for yourself. Now, you can send her a link to the online article and bookmark it for yourself.

Projects
If you have several small projects going at once, you could keep the information for all of them in one file, or you might prefer to keep a separate file for each one. If separated, "Project" files should be arranged alphabetically. Those projects that are currently active fall into the action files while those that are completed or have been put "on hold" temporarily go into reference files.

If the project involves many papers, it may be appropriate to have a reference file and an action file. The action file would contain only those papers you need in order to complete the current step of the project. When that step is completed, review the materials in the file, discard what you don't need and return the rest to the reference file. Then, move the papers relating to the next step of the project to the action file.

Special Events
If you enjoy many outings—concerts, lectures, sports events—but have difficulty keeping track of them, you may wish to keep a separate "Events Calendar." When you receive a notice of an upcoming event, list it on that calendar. Be sure, of course, to put definite commitments on your master calendar. Other options are to have a folder labeled "Schedules" into which you put these notices, or to hang them on the bulletin board. Then, if you have a free evening you can check the folder to see what options you have. This is particularly helpful if you have out-of-town guests and you are assisting them in planning their schedules, or you want to entertain them.

One advantage to electronic calendars is that you can add in special events calendars in different colors to see the entire season of theatre shows, for example. With the click of a button, the calendar can be hidden from view, so you only see your actual calendar items.

Take to Office/Home
Designate a particular place to put those papers (and other items) you need to take with you to work. Choose a convenient location—on a table near the door, for example. Try keeping your briefcase in the same spot so that you can put things right into the briefcase. If your briefcase is not in the usual spot, put the item where your briefcase should be. Then, when you return the briefcase to its proper place, it will be easy to get them together. This will stop the frustrating game of having one and not the other, or vice versa. You should also have a similar setup in your office.

Upcoming Meetings/Trips
Virtually every time you plan to go to a meeting or take a trip you will accumulate emails and papers related to that event, whether it is an airplane ticket, a meeting agenda, or an email from a friend asking you to call or visit when you are in the city.

When the trip or meeting is over, get rid of those emails/pieces of paper that are no longer essential and file the remaining emails/papers according to how you will use them next. For example, the email from your friend might contain an address that could be entered in your address book and then the email could be deleted.

Write

Sometimes writing a letter or an email is the next action to take. "Write" includes business letters, personal letters, thank you notes and special occasion cards.

If writing is a problem area for you, take some time to think about what you can do to make the task easier. Many people find it helps to physically separate these categories. Sometimes you may feel like spending 10 minutes writing a thank-you note but not an hour writing an old college roommate on Facebook. If you have to dig through a huge pile of papers or a long list of electronic messages to find what interests you at the moment, you may lose interest before you find it!

I use airport waiting time to shop for greeting cards I like. Because I keep a supply of favorites on hand, sending a handwritten congratulations card literally takes only minutes—and I'm sure doing it makes me feel every bit as good as the person to whom I send it! Keep postcards on hand for quick notes if you need them. These days, who doesn't enjoy getting something besides fliers and bills in their mail?

If you are procrastinating about writing a letter, ask yourself if a phone call would suffice, or at least get the process started. Writing an outline for yourself to help organize your thoughts will make the letter or email less difficult to write.

The major advantage to this system of file categories is the increased ability to manage your time effectively. It is a good time-management practice to group like activities together. Then, when you have ten minutes before a business meeting at work, or before you need to meet your child at school, a quick look in "Call" can help you use those ten minutes to your advantage. Or, if you're going to an appointment where you may have to wait, take along "Write" with some stationery for personal notes or some scratch paper or your laptop to draft more formal correspondence.

Logistics/Location

You may be feeling swamped at this point! Anything new can seem overwhelming, so don't despair too early in the game. Try one or two action files to begin—"Calls Waiting" is a favorite of many of my clients.

One question you may have is "Where do I put all these files?" If you're using a computer to create all these, you can save them in the "documents" area. But, if you're an "out of sight, out of mind" person, you might want to keep them saved on your desktop. If you're using paper, there are a variety of file folder containers for manila or hanging files that you can put on top of your desk.

If you prefer the "clean desk look," put them in a filing drawer in your desk, if there is one, or in a portable file box under or near your desk.

As you experiment with the system, you'll discover that each category does not have to be a "file" per se, nor does it have to be on your desk. For example, I know of no one who's "Read" category will fit into a file folder, and most people don't read at their work area. So "Read" could be in a basket beside your easy chair, your bed, or even in the bathroom—or, most likely, a combination (See Chapter 17 for more detailed information on "Read").

All Those Files!

Now, you might be asking "How do I remember to look in all those files?" Just try it! You can put a symbol on your calendar to remind you to look. In many instances, such as "Call," there will undoubtedly be one call you'll automatically remember to make. When you check the file for information on that call, you will be reminded of the others you want to make.

You may be confused with the similarity of the categories for the "To Do" list (Chapter 10) and the action files. Sometimes your "To Do" is just a thought, in which case you write it in your "To Do" book (or on a piece of paper in your action file). Other times, the "To Do" involves a piece of paper that goes in the action file. This does not mean you have to make duplicates, unless you choose to use a duplication system as an insurance policy.

The List - Possible Action Files:

    •Call

    •Calls Expected

    •Computer Entry/Data Entry

    •Discuss

    •File (Use tray instead of folder)

- •Order

- •Pay

- •Pending/Waiting on Responses

- •Photocopy (But only if you really need it!)

- •Project

- •Read

- •Sign

- •Special events (Not a permanent action file.)

- •Take to office/home

- •Upcoming meetings/trips (Not a permanent action file.)

- •Write

Chapter Twelve
Names and Numbers

Now that you have eliminated or filed all the papers you can, using your calendar, your "to do" list, or your action files, all that remains are the items you want to keep for reference. Some of the most crucial of these items are names and numbers — your contact management system.

We used to keep all sorts of extra papers for reference. For example, before, if you were to take a trip to San Francisco and your cousin lives there, you might write him a letter and get his phone number, which you would then keep on the piece of paper or write in your address book. In these days of cell phones and Internet, things have greatly changed. Now, you might send him an email or Facebook message, and save the phone number in your cell phone to call when you arrive.

But what about the business card of the woman you met at the networking event? Where did you put it?

Hemphill's Principle: "If you don't know you have it, or you can't find it, it is of no value to you!"

Many of the pieces of paper floating around our homes are there because they have an important telephone number written or printed on them—or because we are afraid the number might become important to us.

Emergency!
There's a serious side to organizing your numbers. If your child becomes ill from drinking a poisonous substance, you won't have time to sort through a pile of papers for the poison-control center's emergency number. Post such numbers by at least one phone on each floor of the house, and program the number into your cell phone. Include police, fire, poison-control center, work numbers for family members, and any neighbor or friend you might call in an emergency. If you do not keep a landline, it's also important to teach your young children how to call 911 from your cell phone in the event that you are hurt.

The White and the Yellow

In our personal lives telephone numbers can be divided into two basic categories: relatives and close friends with whom we always want to stay in contact regardless of where we live; and neighbors, services, stores, schools, organizations or government agencies with whom we will no longer have contact if we move.

In other words, each of us has a personal "white pages" and a personal "yellow pages." For many people who move frequently, it is essential to separate those two categories, so when they do move it is easy to tear out the "Minneapolis" yellow pages and start "Denver."

The first step in designing a good system for addresses and telephone numbers is to determine whether you wish to divide your "white pages" and your "yellow pages" into separate systems, or use one system. Your choice will be influenced to some extent by the volume of information you want to keep. If you have a career, a family, an active community life, or travel frequently, you may need more than one.

Tips for Saving Time on the Phone

When you make a call:

1. Group calls whenever possible.

2. If you call some people frequently and they're hard to reach, ask when the best time is to call.

3. Identify yourself and why you're calling. For example, "Hi, Jerry." This is Pat Roberts. I'm calling to find out what time our homeowner's meeting is on Friday."

4. If your call is complicated, make an agenda and check items off as you discuss them.

5. If you think you won't cover all the issues, prioritize them and start with the most important.

6. At the end of the call, decide when you will call again or what other way you could get information you may need.

7. If you get an answering machine, leave as complete a message as you can. Repeat your number twice, once at the beginning and once at the end

---

of the message. Avoid phone tag by giving options such as a good time to reach you, or alternate numbers.

When you get a call

1. Use voice mail to decide when to take calls.

2. Use assertive language such as, "What can I do for you?"

3. Be honest! If you don't have time to talk, say so: "I'm sorry, but I can't talk now. When can I call you back?"

Choose Your Names and Numbers System

As of late 2008, 17.5 percent of households depended solely on cell phones for communication and more than 13 percent of households received almost all calls on their cell phones despite owning a landline. A total of 85 percent of Americans own a cell phone.

Because cell phones can store so much data, it's very easy to create new contacts and enter in the information. In addition, because the yellow pages are easily accessible online, many people aren't keeping the same amount of "yellow page" information, choosing instead to do a search each time they need the phone number for a plumber. Doing so enables them to keep only friends, family and a few "yellow page" numbers, such as the doctor's office, in their cell phones.

The type of system you choose is up to you. Some people still prefer a simple loose-leaf notebook or a preprinted telephone and address book. Some smartphones will now sync your email address book online with your cell phone contact list so you can access the information anywhere.

If you already have a system that you've inherited from someone else or yours isn't working well, start over. Don't make "organizing your phone numbers" a project for when you have time. Instead, start with a new file and add the numbers from the old one as you use them.

In making your decision, keep in mind how portable your system needs to be, or whether you plan duplicate systems for office, home (more than one floor), vacation home, or travel. Whatever system you choose, the determining factor in the success of your system is ensuring that you will be able to retrieve the information when you need it.

At home, you should be able to access your complete system from your office or work space. If you are using a paper system, consider where you make your calls at home and make sure you keep the numbers you need in the right location. For example, I frequently make telephone calls to family members from my bedroom, but nearly always make business-related calls from my office area. (Yes, there will be times when the number you need will be in the wrong place, but remember that organization isn't about perfection, just progress.)

Be sure you have your most frequently used numbers programmed into your cell phone, so you have access to the numbers when you're away from home or at the office.

Hemphill's Principle: "If you don't know you have it, or you can't find it, it is of no value to you!"

But How Can I Find It?

The major advantage of an email or cell phone system for recording names and numbers is that searching for them is relatively simple. Many email address books have a "notes" section where you can put all kinds of details, such as where you met someone, who introduced you, etc. In some programs, even that section is keyword searchable, which means that the more information you put in, the more ways you can find it.

If you want to go electronic, but it is new to you, be sure to use a system that is web-based, meaning you can access it online from anywhere. If it is only stored locally on your computer's hard drive, it won't help you when you are away from your laptop. The best systems will sync your email address book with your cell phone. Also, don't forget that financial management programs such as Quicken or Microsoft Money come with an address book, as do email programs such as Outlook Express.

Don't assume that all information should be recorded in the same way. You might list a number by the name of the individual, the name of the company or organization, the type of service they perform, or in rare instances, perhaps even by the name of the person who introduced you.

Sometimes you may wish to record numbers in more than one category. For example, you might have one card for Household Repairs on which you list several services. However, you might also have a separate card for "Pipewrench, Peter—Plumber," or "Plumber—Peter Pipewrench." In general though, the simpler the system is the more inclined you will be to use it. Ask yourself the question, "What word would I think of if I wanted to contact this person?" Use that answer as your key word for entering the information into your system.

Business Cards

These days, a lot of the paper piles are business cards. I hear questions about business cards all the time. No one wants to sit and type the information from 54 business cards into his or her Outlook address book. The simple truth about these pieces of paper is that they are the same as any other paper in your home. You must File, Act or Toss each time you receive a business card.

In my experience, we keep far more business cards than we should – simply because we don't want to throw them away. But ask yourself: Am I really going to call this person? If I need to get in touch with him/her, do I know someone who has this information? If the answers are no and yes, it's an easy toss. As I have said, today's mail is tomorrow's pile. If you enter the information from each business card as you receive it, you will only spend two minutes doing so. If you wait until you have a stack, it will take much longer.

You can also scan the information. Some scanners are made specifically for business cards, and some paper scanners will also handle them. Or, you can use a service such as Shoeboxed (http://www.shoeboxed.com/), which will scan in your receipts and business cards for you.

The Rotary Card File

If you prefer to keep phone numbers on paper and don't need to be as mobile, the rotary card file is still one of the best systems for keeping numbers organized. (Rolodex® is the most common brand, but Bates, Eldon and Rubbermaid also make them.)

I recommend purchasing a card file that uses 3" x 5" cards. They are large enough to staple or tape business cards directly onto (that way you don't have to copy the information) and provide enough room to give you plenty of writing space.

A standard format will make your rotary system easier to use. Put the key word—an individual's name (last name first), or the name of the organization, business or service—in the upper left-hand corner and the phone number in the upper right, as this is the information you will need most often. Then, list the address under the key word. If the person has other phone numbers—the home number of a business acquaintance or a company's fax number, for example—record these numbers as well. Be sure to note which number is which.

In addition to name, address, and telephone number, the rotary card file can be used for recording other useful information about that person or business: key people at a business, a simple record of correspondence or telephone exchanges, birthdays, anniversaries, and dates of special events.

It is also the perfect place to record bits of information you'd like to have at your fingertips, such as the Social Security numbers for your family, or the combination to your child's bike lock. If you're not worried about security, you could also list all of your credit card numbers with the number to call in case they are lost or stolen. Think of the file as a "mini-file" for odd bits of information—a place to put information too small for a traditional file folder.

Don't assume that all names and numbers information should be recorded in the same way. You might list a number by the name of the individual, the name of the company or organization, the type of service they perform, or in rare instances, perhaps even by the name of the person who introduced you.

Today's Mail Is Still Tomorrow's Pile

If you have a system that doesn't work—or no system at all—begin one immediately. If you put it aside as a big project, for "when things calm down," you are unlikely to ever accomplish the task. Instead, start the new system with the next phone number you use. In the beginning, use two systems at once, such as rotary file and your cell phone/email address book. As you pull information out of the rotary file, put each bit of information into your email address book. Eventually, you can combine the two systems into one, or the old one will become so old you will feel comfortable throwing it away.

Chapter Thirteen
Your Reference Files

Research shows that 80 percent of the papers in most files are never used.

One of the most frequent scenarios seen on the TV shows today about packrats and hoarders relate to boxes of papers with articles. Here's how it happens! You're reading something and you want to save it. In the past, you would tear the article out of the newspaper or magazine and file it in your reference files. Now, you may just bookmark the online article to read later.

Either way, you're creating reference files, a place to keep things you might want to use later. Research shows that 80 percent of the papers in most files are never used and that the average person keeps 3,000 emails in his/her inbox. With so much information available online, you can find almost anything later. So, before you save that email or file that piece of paper, ask yourself, "What's the worst thing that could happen?"

Recently I read an article about a couple who had both been "downsized" and were looking for ways to save money. As they were considering options, they discovered they could easily have a two-bedroom house instead of a three-bedroom house because one room was full of paper they never used!

Of course, there are some items you want to keep. And, you can keep everything you want – if you're willing to pay the price: time, space, money, and energy! But don't forget Hemphill's Principle: "If you don't know you have it, or you can't find it, it is of no value!"

When it comes to paper, if you have a filing system that isn't working or if you inherited someone else's system, read this chapter and start over. Don't try to fix the existing files. Instead, incorporate the information from the old system into the new system as you need it.

So what is filing? Really, what you're doing is determining what files need to be grouped together: Should you take out all the files that are related to taxes and put them in a special category called "Financial?" What should you call a particular file—"car," "automobile" or "Nissan?"

Computer Filing

Whether you're using a Mac or PC, you're probably saving some documents and files on your computer. The beauty of this is that you can use the search function to track down those documents if you can't remember where you put them. As mentioned earlier, be sure you're backing up those files. Put the files in the same categories and use the same names as you would with your paper system. That way, when you're searching for your checking statement, you know which file it's in – whether you're looking for the most recent electronic copy or the old paper version.

Some great computer tools for keeping track of your reference items:

- Delicious bookmarks- This allows you to bookmark, or save, the URL of a page you'd like to keep. You can name it and add tags to help you search for it later. These can be shared with your friends or marked "private." It's web-based, so if you're on someone else's computer, you can still get to your favorite pages by logging in to your delicious account. You can find a list of other bookmarking tools by searching for "bookmarking" online.
- Evernote - Another web-based program, Evernote is a place to store notes in text, audio or picture form.
- Instapaper - A program for your iPhone and Mac that allows you to save articles to read later.

These are just a few programs, and more are always coming.

I personally use a cloud computing solution called PBWorks for storing all my electronic files, indexing paper files, and keeping a household inventory. It allows me to have "workspaces" where I can share information with family, financial advisors, medical care providers, church committees, and colleagues. It also automatically backs up documents in the cloud. With the software, you can also automatically cross-reference your files with as many words or phrases as you like, easily share information with others, identify a specific date when you want to review a file and, most importantly, find what you're looking for in seconds. Plus, there is no space limit.

For more information, go to www.BarbaraHemphill.com.

Most of us have both paper and electronic reference files. If you're going Almost Paperless™, you might consider scanning your paper files into your computer, but that depends on your preference and how much paper you have. If you are going to do this, again, don't try to tackle the whole thing at once. Instead, every time you reach into your files for something, take the time then to scan it and save it in the new format.

Whether you decide to use the computer, web-based software or stick with a traditional filing system, the components of an effective reference file are still the same:

- •Management
- •Mechanics
- •Maintenance

In my work with clients, I frequently discover that two of these three factors are already in operation. As soon as the third factor, Maintenance, is incorporated, their system starts to work.

File Management

One reason people resist filing papers away is a fear that they will make a poor decision and file the paper in an inappropriate or hard-to-remember file. Here are some guidelines that will help you with your filing decisions – whether for electronic or paper.

Ask yourself, "Under what circumstances would I want this information?"

Be specific! "Just in case" won't help you find it again. If the answer is, "I might want this information if I were writing a speech," then the information should be saved in a "Speech Ideas" file. If you answer, "I'll need this when I sell the house," then a "House—Main Street" file might be a good choice.

Ask yourself, "If I wanted this information, what word would first enter my mind?"

The answer to that question will tell you what reference file is appropriate for this piece of paper. For example, a flier about ordering candy from a specialty company could be filed under "Gift Ideas" or "Mail Order Information." And invitations from a past party could be filed under "Party Ideas," "Printing Ideas" or "Mementos."

File information according to how you will use it, not where you got it.

For example, your local homeowner's association published an article recommending repair services in the area. Suppose you wake up one morning to discover that you have no hot water. What are the chances you'd remember that article in the "Homeowner's Association" file? A file labeled "Services—Household Repair" might be more useful. If you prefer unorthodox names for files, you might call it something like "Uh-oh," to mean things have gone wrong and you need help.

Put all papers in their most general category first. For example, try keeping all of your warranties and instructions in a single file. Then, if the file becomes too bulky, break it down into "Warranties and Instructions—Appliances," "Warranties and Instructions—Clothing," etc.

With both paper and electronic folders, it's easier to look through one file with 20 items than 10 files with two items in each; fewer places to look means fewer places to lose. The added advantage is that when you are using a file to get a particular paper or document, you may also discover other documents you have forgotten. As a result you will be able to use more of the information that you file.

If a paper or document can be filed in more than one place, choose the one you are most likely to look in first.

With electronic filing, you might be less inclined to file in an organized manner because you can always type in search terms and find the document no matter where you put it. I still encourage you to file in a system that makes sense to you. If you know where the file is, it's easier to find it without taking the time to do a search.

If you're dealing with paper files, you may want to write a note on the other file folders that says, "See also. . ." With electronic files, it's tough to squeeze that into the folder name. You might just need to think more carefully about where you file.

Organize your files consistently.
For example, you may have medical and educational records for several members of the family. Decide whether you want all of John's files together; i.e., "John—Education," "John—Medical," or all medical files together, i.e., "Medical—Ann," "Medical—John."

Group like files together.
Whenever you have files that you want to keep together physically in your file system, find a word that encompasses all the files. For example, instead of having a file that says "Biking" under "B" and "Skiing" under "S," you could have "Recreation—Biking" and "Recreation—Skiing."

File Index
A file index is the final and perhaps the most important step in managing your paper files, because the same information can be filed several ways. For example, I could file information about my car in "Automobile," "Car," "Chrysler," or "Vehicle." The problem comes if you file information under "Car" one time, and under "Chrysler" the next—and your spouse looks for it under "Automobile"!

This dilemma can be avoided by making an alphabetical list of all file names, cross referenced to files that contain related material. When you are writing or typing the index, leave space between each letter of the alphabet so you will have room to add new file names as you need them. Put as many names on one page as possible; use columns if necessary. It's unlikely you'll ever get to the filing if you have to read a 15-page guide first! (See the sample file index at the end of this chapter. Use this sample as your starting point by crossing out categories you won't need and adding in those you will.)

Keep your file index accessible in hard copy in the very front of your filing system or at your desk, and make changes to it with pen or pencil. Or, keep the list on your computer so you can update it quickly and easily. When you read an article you want to file, check the index to see what files already exist that might be appropriate for that particular article.

Use the index if you are looking for an article. It is much easier to check a file index to see where you might find an article than it is to open the file drawer and go through all of your files.

The index is particularly important if you are learning a new system or if more than one person will be using the same system. Keep in mind that if there is a particular piece of paper you are afraid of losing, you can list it on the index. For example, "Birth Certificate"—See "Legal Information."

For computer files, some find it unnecessary to keep a file index, because you can search for the item by keyword. Either way, be sure to name your documents by a keyword you are likely to remember.

Sample Headings for Your System

You may wish to organize your files into various categories. A friend of mine divides her files into three categories: Financial and legal, reference, and children. Some people put all files that involve payments of any kind into one category and all other files into another reference category.

Be aware that there will always be gray areas when you begin categorizing. For example, you might think of "Medical" as a reference file or a financial file. You can eliminate the problem of determining what category a file should be in by filing everything strictly by the alphabet. Then, if you are looking for "Medical," there is no question of where to look.

Remember that your filing system will change as your life circumstances change. For example, if you get married, you will need to decide whether to maintain two separate filing systems or combine them into one. If you decide to combine them, you may want to use colors to identify files that belong specifically to each person. (Color-coding can also cause problems, as discussed later in this chapter.)

File Mechanics

The importance of the mechanics of a filing system is often overlooked. Very few people enjoy paper filing; most can't stand it! Here are three main reasons:

•They dislike deciding where to file the papers;
•They dislike the physical discomfort of jamming hands into overstuffed file drawers; or
•They dislike the annoyance of looking into numerous file drawers before they find the file they need.

If you are comfortable with computers and dislike filing for those reasons, then you might consider going Almost Paperless™. Filing your documents is as easy as a few mouse clicks and you may find it less irksome than paper filing. However, since most of us still have some paper, there are other ways to make filing less irritating.

Your File Cabinet

Selecting the right file cabinet is important. My first choice, without a doubt, is a good-quality full-suspension file cabinet. Full suspension means that you can open the drawers all the way so no files are obstructed from view.

There are two types of file cabinets, vertical and lateral, which are distinguished by how they open. Vertical cabinets are generally 28" high, 15" wide and 26" deep. The drawer pulls out to the full depth of the cabinet, and files are arranged from front to back. Lateral file cabinets are generally 28" high and 18" deep and come in widths of 30", 36", or 42". The depth is approximately 35" when the drawer is open, and the files can be arranged front to back in rows or side-to-side. If not in stock, any good office supply store will have more options online or in a catalog in which you can see pictures of the various options.

For most households, a two-drawer, full-suspension vertical cabinet will be enough. If you want to create additional working space in your work area, a two-drawer full-suspension lateral file would be a good choice. If you want or need more filing space, you can purchase a four or five-drawer file.

You can find less expensive file cabinets at a discount store, but I don't recommend them for files you use frequently. If you cannot afford a full-suspension file, you may find that filing boxes are more accessible than a poorly made metal cabinet. Keep in mind that a good quality file cabinet is a lifetime investment. Prices vary dramatically, so comparison shop after you find the cabinet you want.

If you don't have room for a traditional filing cabinet or you feel it doesn't fit with your interior decor, other options range from cardboard or plastic file boxes to solid wood cabinets designed to coordinate with your furniture. Portable file folders work well if you use your kitchen or dining room table as a workspace and want to bring the files with you when you work. They also work well for files that you need access to only occasionally, and can store in the basement, attic, garage or some other out-of-the-way place.

Your Choice of File Folders
You might be surprised to discover that another big decision is what kind of file folders you will use. There are several options, including some file systems that are ready to go, right out of the box, with labels and a file index.

"Hanging Files," made by Pendaflex (www.Pendaflex.com) are my preference, because they are well made and the glue along the tops will not come undone. Although they are more expensive than manila folders, they will last significantly longer, and the plastic stand-up tabs make the labels much easier to read. If your filing cabinet doesn't accommodate hanging files, you can purchase a hanging-file frame that can be sized to fit your file drawer.

It is not necessary to put manila file-folders inside the hanging files, but there are a few situations when that is advisable to do so. Sometimes, you may need to take material away from your home or office to use it. For example, you could use a manila folder to keep a file for a committee on which you serve so you can take the information in the folder with you to the meeting. If you do use two folders, label the hanging file and the manila file identically. This will make it easy to return the file to its proper place.

You could also use manila folders in a hanging file when you need to make subdivisions within the file. For example, the hanging folder could be labeled "Car," and the manila folders could be labeled "Car Insurance," "Car Repairs," etc.

If you're using manila files, buy the kind that are reinforced across the top. They will last longer, and cause fewer paper cuts. You can also crease the fold lines at the bottom of the folder to increase its capacity and prevent obstruction of the file label.
Another type is the "Box-Bottom" file, which is useful for very thick files, or a file that has many subdivisions. These have a one-half to three-inch cardboard strip along the bottom of the file.

Hanging folders come in a variety of colors, as do other types of file folders. The hanging folders sometimes come with colored plastic tabs, and in the case of the darker colors, such as red or blue, you may prefer to substitute clear plastic labels that are easier to read, particularly if you used typed labels.
Plastic tabs can go on the front or back of hanging files. Most people put them on the back, probably because it is consistent with the label on the back of manila folders. Try putting them on the front instead. The big advantage of having the label on the

front is that when you are filing a piece of paper and you grab the plastic tab the file automatically opens to the place you need to file the paper. You can use whichever method you prefer; just be consistent.

There are also many other kinds of file folders available. If you have shelf space rather than a file cabinet, use file folders with labels on the narrow end instead of on the top. That way you can put your files on shelves and still see the labels easily.
Some people like to use file folders with metal fasteners so that the papers can be punched and put in the file in chronological order and will stay that way. In most instances I find that the results are not worth the effort. Over and over again, I have seen filing pile up because it took too much time and effort to get the holes punched.

Able Labels
Labeling is the key to any effective filing system. Often I find files with penciled labels—or no label at all because they are only "temporary" files. Often, files become like the "temporary" building on my college campus that served as the music building for 27 years! It is very simple to use peel-off file labels so that if you need to change the label you can do so easily. In the meantime, you have a file that is easy to find.

As previously discussed in "File Management," determine what the label should say by asking yourself: "If I wanted this information again what word would I think of?"

Even though I am a proficient typist, I prefer to handwrite my file labels because they're easier to read. I find that printing labels in capital letters creates the most consistent, readable appearance. But, if your handwriting isn't so great, portable label printers are widely available at prices starting at $50. These are excellent for labeling all kinds of items around your household. If you hand write your labels, use a dark-colored felt-tipped pen of medium thickness, and make sure to print clearly so that others can read the headings. One client attaches a pen on a string inside the file cabinet so the pen is always there when she wants it.

Using Color
Some people like to color-code their files, and there are lots of ways to do so. You could use colored file folders, colored file labels, colored dots to stick on labels, or colored pens to write the labels. Color is very useful if it tells a story. For example, you could use red labels on any files that contain information you will need at tax time, or you could use a different color label or file folder for each member of the family.

Color can also be confusing if it's not used consistently, and very frustrating when you want to make a file quickly but can't find the right color label, pen or dot. I would caution you to use color sparingly unless you have someone to help you with the file mechanics or you particularly enjoy doing it yourself.

For that reason, I urge you not to buy a box of multicolored file folders. I have seen many people do this, but most don't have a plan for how to use that color. It often causes more disorganization.

Whatever type of file folder you choose, put the key word at the left of the label when writing or typing labels. For example, "Education—John—2002" rather than "2002—Education—John." And beware of the "just for now" trap! Keep the system simple enough so that you can easily maintain it as you go.

Too Many Systems
One of the temptations—and most frequent mistakes—in setting up a filing system is to create too many systems. In doing this you create more work for yourself. If you are looking for information, you first have to remember which filing system it is in and then determine where it is within the system. If you are trying to file information, you may find it difficult to determine which system is appropriate for that information. Unless there is a clear-cut identity, such as all of the files involving financial information, keep all files together in one A-Z system. Then, if you are looking for "Entertaining," you will go directly to "E," instead of wondering whether you put it in the "personal" files or the "house" files.

Special Mechanics Tips
Here are some additional tips that will make the mechanics of your filing easier:
- •Avoid using paper clips in files. They take up more space, and more importantly, catch on other papers when you file them, obstructing the file label. Instead, use staples to keep together papers that are related. Also, keep a staple remover handy.
- •File papers so that the most recent ones are at the front. When you open the file you can immediately see the latest action or information. This will also make cleaning the file less time-consuming because the oldest information will automatically be at the back.
- •Arrange the file folders alphabetically. Try this idea even if you've resisted it in the past. You'll be surprised by how much more quickly you will be able to find the file you need.
- •Label the outside of the file cabinet as to its contents, either by subject or by alphabet. This will save you from opening the third drawer when the file you want is in the second.

File Maintenance
No matter how much time and energy you spend creating a system to fit your particular needs, you will still need to adopt a plan to maintain the system. The following steps will help:

Determine when—or if—you will do the filing. More and more professional people are recognizing that it is cost effective to hire someone else to do the routine household management tasks—including filing—just as we hire others to maintain the lawn.

If you will be doing your own filing, decide how you will keep the "File" pile from becoming larger than the file cabinet. Some people file when they pay bills, that way two potentially unpleasant tasks are done at the same time, and they can reward themselves with a more pleasant activity when they're finished. Other people wait until the "File" tray is full.

People procrastinate about filing because they don't like deciding where the paper should be filed. That decision is easier to make when you have just read the letter or article. Remember that if you circle the keyword or write it in the upper right hand corner before you put the paper in the "To File" tray or your "File" action file, the filing task will be only a mechanical one and will take less time.

This method is essential if someone else does your filing, because no two people would necessarily put a paper in the same file. A paper relating to your car insurance, for example, could be filed under "Car" or "Insurance." In this instance, the File Index again becomes invaluable.

Clean out files as you use them.
I cannot count how many times I've seen clients with a paper in hand that they knew could be tossed say, "I'll have to clean this out someday," and promptly put the piece of paper back into the file again instead of directly into the recycle bin! Why not just toss old files as you come across them?

Establish an annual "File Clean-Out Day."
Around tax time is a good choice, since you will be looking into many of your files at that time anyway. An alternative is to wait until you need the file space. As long as you have room to file papers easily, the issue of purging is not a major one. When you opt not to file because it is physically uncomfortable or downright impossible to get your fingers into the file cabinet, then the time for Clean Out Day has arrived!

How Long Is Enough?
Determine how long you need to keep the papers you file. Date information when you file it so it will be easy to tell if it is recent enough to be useful. In certain cases, such as a file of newsletters, you can put the retention information right on the file label. For example, "Community Newsletter—Keep one year."

The issue of retention guidelines is a difficult one. In many instances the decision is purely discretionary. How long do you want to keep articles you intend to read or reviews of restaurants? In other cases, you should simply keep material forever, updating the information as necessary. This would include birth certificates, wills, insurance policies, school and medical records, etc.

There are legal reasons for keeping other material for a certain amount of time. This material mostly deals with financial and tax matters. For quick reference to see how long you should keep what, check out the appendix.

There are also other factors to consider in making your decision about retaining material. One is space. If you have enough of it (say a basement) to keep everything—and it doesn't make you feel uncomfortable to have that paper lying around—then ignore it. Be sure the material is well organized—and that you separate the "archival materials" from those you are currently using.

Even if you have ample room for storage, if you get a knot in your stomach every time you open the file drawer or closet door, the price you are paying for your failure to make decisions about paper retention is too high, and you should look for alternatives.

The following is a list of the kinds of information that can be put in a home filing system. Detailed information about what could go into the files can be found in later chapters. The categories here are listed alphabetically, as you would file them. As you read about categories you could use—and think of others that are not listed here—jot them down.

Categories

- Art Owned — Could also be filed under "Personal Property" or "Insurance."

- Articles — This could be divided into categories by subject, e.g. "Articles—Psychology."

- Book Information — This could be divided into categories such as "Books—Novels," "Books—History" etc.

- Car Maintenance — Keep copies of all receipts from work done on your car, along with the manual that came with the car when you bought it. Information could also be filed under

"Automobile" or by the make of the car.

- Child-care Information – Include summer camp information and photocopies of blank forms to be filled out with information for the sitter. Information could also be filed under "Babysitter" or "Camp."

- Church/Synagogue — This could be listed under specific name: "Calvary Church," or "Temple Zion," for example.

- Consumer Information — If this file becomes too bulky, divide it into categories such as "Consumer Information—Electronics," Consumer Information—Real Estate," etc.

- Credit Cards — For each account, enter card number, address, and phone number to call if card is lost. (Keep a duplicate copy of the list in your safe deposit box.)

- Death Information — What to do in case of your death or a relative's. Include a copy of wills. (Originals should be kept with your attorney or in a fireproof box. In some states a safe deposit box may be sealed upon your death.)

- Diet Information — This could also be placed under "Health" or "Nutrition."

- Entertainment — Put ideas for outings for family or house guests. This could be divided into categories.

- Education Records — Make one file for each member of family.

- Financial Records — Separate general financial planning information from your personal information. This file could contain information about loans, mortgages, investments, etc.

- Gardening and Plants

- Gift Ideas

- Hobbies — Divide into specific areas such as "Gardening," "Coins," etc.

- Holidays — File ideas for gifts, a record of gifts given, ideas for next year, copies of the annual letter you send to friends and family, etc.

- Home Decorating – Divide into specific areas if too bulky for one file.

- Household Maintenance Records

- Humor — Favorite cartoons, jokes, articles.

- Income Tax Information — Divide this file into sub-files for each tax year. Keep all of the records you may need in case of an audit. These include records of donations, taxes paid, and receipts for any tax-deductible items (See Chapter 16 for information on how long you need to keep these records).

- Insurance — You may need several files for this important category. Keep one for "Car," another for "Household/Personal Property" (including receipts for art, jewelry, furs, etc.), a third for "Life Insurance" and a fourth for "Medical Insurance," which in turn could be broken down into three folders—"Bills to Be Submitted" (keep blank forms here), "Bills Submitted But Not Paid," and "Bills Paid."

- Inventory — List items in various storage areas of your home or in other locations.

- IRA – This information could be included in "Retirement Information," or perhaps with "Financial Records."

- Party Records — Guest lists, menus of past parties, and ideas for future ones.

- Personal Property — Specifics on valuable items owned, if not already in Insurance file.

- Quotes and Favorite Articles — This could also be called "Speech Ideas" if you make frequent public appearances.

- Recreation — This file can be divided into various sports and activities.

- Resume

- Retirement Information — Keep your latest pension statement here. If you are enrolled in other pension plans from former employers, also keep information on those accounts here. IRA and Keogh statements could be filed here as well.

- Safe Deposit Box — Keep a list of what is located there. Also use this file for temporary storage of items to take to your safe deposit box.

- Services — This file could be divided into "Personal" and "Household" for information such as hair stylist, physical therapist, plumber, electrician, etc.

- Shopping Information – Mail-order information, clippings about new stores, and brochures are filed here.

- Special Interests — Divide this file into categories such as "History," "Psychology."

- Subscriptions and Memberships — Keep records of renewals and order forms here.

- Stocks, Bonds and Mutual Funds — Divide into separate sub-files for each investment you own. Keep broker statements here, along with annual reports. Also make a separate file here for information on stocks, bonds or mutual funds you're considering buying.

- Travel — If you have a lot of information here, divide the file by geographic areas.

- Warranties and Instructions — If this file becomes too bulky, use a box-bottom file (as discussed earlier in this chapter) or divide it into types, e.g., "Major Appliances," "Lawn Tools," or "Home Electronics."

Chapter Fourteen

Bills, Bills, Bills

We can laugh about many of the papers in our lives, but there is little humor in unpaid bills. A lost bill can mean a disconnected telephone or a cold house in December. Bills can represent emotionally charged issues such as the extravagant new suit that you've never worn or the vacation that fizzled.

We must not only deal with the issue of finding the money to pay bills, but we must also determine who pays them—when, where, and how. Frequently clients spend more time debating whether to postpone paying a bill than it would have taken for them to write the check. And how embarrassing it is when the mortgage company calls about your delinquent payment and you can't even find your checkbook!

Keeping Track - Paper

You can reduce the stress of paying bills by establishing a method to keep track of them. If you still receive your bills via snail mail, the simplest method is to put all the bills in one place, pay them once a month, and then file all the receipts in one place, or in different places depending on the type of expense involved. Then, if you need to refer to the payment, you will be able to find the information.

Using this method, it is not necessary to open a bill at the time you receive it. In fact, unless you plan to do something specific with the information in the bill at that time, I don't particularly recommend it. The result of just opening many bills without acting on them is a significant increase in the number of pieces of paper you have to handle. More importantly, you increase the likelihood that the bill and its return envelope will get separated.

If you're not going to pay all the bills at one time, you need a good method to keep track of when to pay them. One method is to separate your bills into two groups based on when they are due. Use your first paycheck of the month to pay the set due soonest, and use your second paycheck of the month to pay the ones with later due dates. If that does not work for you, try opening them and marking the amount due and the due date on the front of the envelope. Then, put a note on your calendar on the day you need to pay the bill. Still another method is to make a list of the bills as they come in. Then you can check them off as you pay them, noting the date paid and the check number. This list can also be useful for future reference.

Many people keep track of their expenses. This book is not intended to be a financial-planning guide; there are several good resources on that subject at your local bookstore or library. The issue of tracking expenses as it relates to paper management, however, has to do with when (and where) you will record your expenses. Decide whether you will enter the information in your budget book when you pay bills, or if that is an unrealistic expectation. If it is, determine when you will enter your expenses, just as you determined when you would pay your bills. Make an appointment with yourself and mark it in your calendar until you're in the habit of recording the information without a reminder.

Keeping Track - Almost Paperless™
The problem with paying bills is that it must be done – by someone. If you hate doing it, do not assume that you have to be that someone. Your spouse might not mind handling the job. Many people hire others, such as a bookkeeper or a professional organizer, to pay bills and handle other routine chores for them, so that they have time and energy for other activities that are more fun (and maybe profitable, thus providing funds to pay for the service).

If, however, you don't have the luxury of someone else to help you pay your bills, what can you do to make the task more palatable? Undoubtedly the greatest inroad the computer industry has made into our homes is the area of managing finances. People who have had little interest in a computer are often motivated when they discover the power of using it to pay bills and keep track of their financial situation.

In Chapter 6, we touched on paying bills online. Let's talk about that in more detail. The first step to going paperless with your bills is to stop the actual inflow of paper. Do an online search for that biller's website – even if it's the city water service – and see if you can switch to paperless bills. This means you will receive an email copy of your bill each month instead of mailed paper. Sometimes billers will advertise paperless billing on the envelope. Many businesses are encouraging paperless billing because it saves them paper and postage costs. Another advantage to this system is that the biller may email you payment reminders if the bill is overdue.

Next, you must figure out a way to pay that bill without the envelope. Of course, you can still write a check and send it in your own envelope, but then you must keep that biller's address. Instead, if you're going Almost Paperless™, your best system is to set up online payments. These can be charged to a credit card, paid through an intermediary system such as PayPal or withdrawn directly from your bank account. If you're going to each individual biller's website to set up payments, you can also set up automatic withdrawals to make sure the bill is always paid. However, if you're not sure of your finances in a particular month, that may not be a good idea.

Going to multiple websites each time to pay a bill can be more tedious than writing out seven checks and mailing them. These days, most banks offer online bill payments. The next time you login, check out this feature. It takes a few minutes to set up each biller (and you will probably need a copy of your bill to do so), but once it's set up, the bank will email you reminders, deliver the bill to you and allow you to click and pay it all in one place.

Regardless of whether you use paper or electronic bill payment systems, be sure to determine the best time for you to pay bills. Do you prefer to pay them once or twice a month, or to pay each one as it arrives?

In the interest of financial planning, it is wiser to pay bills once a month. This method gives you the opportunity to look at your overall financial picture and make financial decisions based on hard facts, rather than on feelings and fears. For example, if you know you can't pay off the balance on all of your credit card bills, pay the one with the highest interest rate first.

However, if you know yourself well enough to recognize that you will procrastinate on a task that feels overwhelming—that is, facing a mountain of bills all at once—you may be better off paying each bill as it comes in.

A Place to Pay Up
If you pay your bills at home, choose where you will do it. If you are going to pay bills as they arrive, the location where you'll pay them must be convenient; otherwise it will be too much trouble to go there and you will not do it consistently.

If you pay bills once or twice a month, it is essential that you have a convenient place to put your "Pay" action file so you can put bills in the folder as they come in and you're sorting the mail. This doesn't necessarily have to be the same place where you will eventually pay the bills.

Be sure to have everything you need in your bill-paying location—stamps, a pen that works, your checkbook, return address labels, envelopes, and a place to put the receipts from the paid bills.

For those paying bills electronically, you'll be using your computer to pay the bills, so you're most likely do so in your home office or business center. Depending on which email program you use, it is best to create a system to mark which emails are bills that must be paid. You can also create a folder for those emails – but be careful! If you are an "out of sight, out of mind" person, it may be easier to keep those bills in your inbox (your "action" file) until they are paid. However, if you are paying your bills online through your bank (and you log in regularly), you may not need to keep the email as a visual reminder.

If you are paying with paper, be sure to get the stamped bills to a place where you will see them so they actually get to the mailbox. Frequently amid my clients' piles of papers, I find checks they wrote but never mailed. Failure to mail a payment can cause frustration and confusion when you receive a delinquency notice for a bill you thought you'd paid. Your check register indicates you paid it. You remember writing the check. Did it get lost in the mail? Did the company make a mistake? Only when your bank statement arrives, or when you call the company, can you know for sure whether or not you paid the bill. And, if it turns out you haven't made the payment, you also have to pay past due penalties.

If you pay bills at the office, establish a system for getting the bills from your mailbox at home to the office. Put them in a basket near the door, in a file on your desk, or directly into your briefcase. You can also arrange to have the bills mailed directly to your office.

Billing Statements: To Save or Not to Save

After you have paid the bills, you've got to do something with the statements. Ask yourself: "Why would I need this statement?" If you recall your past habits, you may realize that you have indeed never used the information. You might then decide to shred the statements, knowing that you can always refer to your canceled checks and check register.

You could also keep a record of payments to a particular company, in case there are billing questions. Put the statements in a reference file marked "MasterCard," or "Sears," or a more generic file, such as "Bills Paid."

Another function of such a file would be to provide a record of personal expenses. For example, if you are divorced, you may keep records of expenditures on children in case a problem develops with child support. If so, create a reference file called "Child Support," "Children," or "Financial Information—Children."

You may need to keep certain statements for specific, but temporary, circumstances. For example, if you plan to sell your home within the next year, keep the utility bills because the information will interest a potential buyer.

Frequently, the primary reason for keeping the information is "for the IRS." If that is the case, see the next chapter for more detailed information.

Receipts: Trash or Treasure

Then there are the humble credit card and ATM receipts—those flimsy little pieces of paper which you often find stuffed in your suit pockets, lying on top of your dresser, and buried in your briefcase or desk drawers. What should you do with them?

Keep in mind that the main purpose of those credit card receipts is to make sure you have been billed properly, and to use as proof of purchase in the event you need to make a return or exchange. If you don't plan to go back and check your statements against your receipts and you don't intend to return the item, then you probably don't need to save the receipt.

However, some receipts must be retained for tax and other financial record-keeping purposes. Other reasons you should keep a receipt include major purchases which have a warranty, tax-deductible items, or a property improvement expense.

In that case, one simple method to organize receipts is to get several business-sized envelopes—one for each credit card. Put the name of one card on each envelope and, if you have the space, hang the envelopes on a bulletin board with the flap tucked inside to create a pocket. When you return home, put receipts in the appropriate envelopes. When the credit card bills arrive, you can match them up with the receipts in minutes and pay the bills (this method also works well for bank statements).

Reduce Your Paper

One way to reduce the paper in your life is to keep fewer credit cards. You'll also save on annual fees. Try to pay off credit card bills monthly, so you don't pay non-deductible interest. If you must carry a balance, make sure your card has a low interest rate. If you own a home, consider a home equity loan, the interest on which is most likely tax deductible. Debit cards are very popular now, eliminating the need to carry a checkbook and create paper checks. They are accepted like a credit card, but debit the amount directly from your account. Just be sure to keep track.

Chapter Fifteen

The Paper Population

Many people fail in setting up new systems because they do not allow enough time to develop the new habits that are necessary to make any kind of change in their life.

You can manage every piece of paper and every electronic document in your life by using the techniques described in the previous chapters.

But, even if you're Almost Paperless™ with your bills, most of your mail, essential documents and your reading materials, there are still more papers. They seem to multiply like mushrooms all over the house—coupons, fliers from local businesses, and instruction books that come with new electronic gadgets, kitchen appliances or garden tools.

Activities like travel, family celebrations, seminars, recreation and sports events create even more paper, and medical emergencies, educational pursuits, career changes, job responsibilities, religious affiliations, club memberships, and community involvement add still more. Many of those groups may be working toward paperless, but usually you end up with at least some paper floating around.

Also contributing to the accumulation are old photographs (before you went digital) and other family mementos, recipes and books. If you receive hard copies of magazines and newspapers, you may have extras lying around or clippings on articles you want to save.

Let us not forget about the papers relating to your children—papers that you need to keep about them, papers they need to keep relating to the management of their own lives, and still more papers you or they want to save as memories of their achievements.

You will undoubtedly have questions about certain pieces of paper, and will discover a variety of ways you could handle them. How do you know which is best?

No Right or Wrong Way

Remember, there is no "right" or "wrong" way to organize anything. If you asked three different interior designers to redesign your living room, you would obviously get three different results. You might like all three of the plans, but one of them would probably appeal to you more than the others. If you asked three different people to write a news article about a community event, you would undoubtedly get three different stories. They would probably all be accurate, but each would be colored by the experiences and writing styles of the individual authors.

Paper management has this same variety and flexibility. The next several chapters will discuss some of the major areas of paper management that you will have to face in your life. You will find different approaches for handling these challenges, along with some of the pros and cons for each method. Choose the way that sounds the most feasible to you, and be sure to give it a fair try.

Many people fail in setting up new systems because they do not allow enough time to develop the new habits that are necessary to make any kind of change in their life. Try the new system for a reasonable amount of time—two to three months is usually adequate. If the new system is still not working, ask yourself these questions: "Is the problem that I don't have enough time? If so, what can I do to make the time?" "Am I having problems with the mechanics? If so, who can help me?" "Do I really want to do this? If not, is there anyone else who can do it?" Or, "What would happen if I didn't do it? What would I do then?"

Often, all that is required for success is a modification of the system. Spend some time identifying what you liked about the system you tried and what you did not. With that information, you can move on to make the necessary changes to create a system that will work for you.

Who's in Charge Here?

One of the questions that inevitably arises in every household deals with who is going to manage the paper. There's likely to be a major conflict if no one in the family is willing to do it, or if there's a disagreement about how the paper should be handled.

Communication and negotiation are the keys to success in family paper management. In most households, specific responsibilities are assigned to specific people. One person may pay bills, while another does the filing. Or, a husband and wife may elect to pick a "bill-paying night" and do it together.

If one family member is more skilled in paper management—or more willing to learn—the entire family will benefit. However, if one person generally does the filing, other family members should know something about the system in case that person is ill or absent. In fact, every member of the household will have some papers to handle. Children need to learn to take care of their own papers, to help prepare them to be independent.

As with any attempt at learning something new, you'll discover stumbling blocks. Don't let that stop you! In every organizing process, things will seem to get worse before they get better. A natural outcome of sorting through piles of papers is a renewed awareness that we are not as productive as we would like to be. Concentrate on how you are going to improve the situation now, not what you should have done in the past.

How Does it Make You Feel?
Sometimes my clients have a great deal of difficulty letting go of the excess in their lives, whether it is paper, clothes, kitchen utensils or their children's outgrown toys. If that's true in your case, ask yourself the question, "How does having this make me feel?" If the answer is anything negative—sad, angry, guilty—then decide whether you want to continue to surround yourself with things that make you feel unhappy.

Often our willingness to let go of something increases if we can identify other people who need it more than we do. You can find local Goodwill or Salvation Army stores online, and most communities usually have many other groups that could benefit from things you no longer use.

The clarity of our goals and our willingness to look at the future—instead of dwelling on the past—is another important factor in our ability to make decisions about what we need to keep. If you find yourself unable to make progress with letting go of things you know deep down inside you really don't need, it might be symptomatic of a deeper underlying problem. You may even wish to seek professional help in setting some specific goals in your life.

Disaster-Proof Your Important Papers
In case you have to evacuate your home in an emergency, keep copies of your most vital papers in a portable container you can easily take with you.

Keep original copies of difficult-to-replace documents, such as birth certificates and titles, in a safe deposit box, and make sure the box is held in more than one person's name. While information regarding bank accounts, insurance policies, and investments can be reproduced from account numbers, having immediate access to a hard copy may be helpful.

Most importantly, keep a list of all the documents you have and where they are located. Make sure that family members and those who need access to them know where to find this master list. (In this situation, a cloud computing solution which can be accessed by any computer to get vital information can literally be a lifesaver!)

Vital Records

- Birth certificates and adoption records

- Marriage certificates and divorce decrees

- Driver's licenses

- Passports/Visas/Green cards

- Social Security cards

- Titles, deeds and registrations for property owned

- Wills and trust documents

- Mortgage and loan information

- Insurance policies

- Bank account records

- Investment account records

- Credit card numbers

Be sure to keep contact numbers saved in your cell phone, including doctor, employer/spouse's employer, children's schools, banks, utility companies, alarm system company, and insurance agents.

Chapter Sixteen

The Tax Man Cometh

It's April 7. You haven't seen the top of the dining room in two weeks because shopping bags and shoeboxes full of paid bills and receipts, piles of canceled checks, and unidentified cash register receipts cover it. There are more receipts in the bottom of your briefcase, the back of the dresser drawer and on your kitchen counter.

To add to the chaos, you've got a 15-page guide from your accountant with instructions on what information he or she needs. Your head pounds and your stomach churns as the countdown begins to April 15. What can you do to minimize the stress around this deadline?

Someone once said that to live comfortably, it's not how much you earn, but how much you keep after taxes. You might hate to pay them, think the system is unfair, dislike the forms, and stage a mini-tax rebellion, but in the end the tax man cometh— sometimes with a penalty!

Two Kinds of Taxpayers
First, it's important to recognize that there are basically two kinds of taxpayers—those who feel comfortable only if they record deductions as they occur during the year and those who prefer to ignore the entire issue until the fear of the penalty for late payment is greater than their willingness to procrastinate.

Somewhere in our education about managing our financial affairs we heard the message that the right way to keep tax records is on a daily, or at least somewhat regular, basis. We envision a professional-looking ledger with neat entries and accurate totals at the end of each month. Most of all, we dream of walking into the tax accountant's office the first week of February with everything in order!

There are many ways to maintain tax information. One man I know files all his receipts in two huge garbage bags—one labeled "Tax Deductible" and the other "Non-Tax Deductible." He then ignores the issue of taxes until the deadline hovers over him and he's forced to dig in.

Most people require a slightly more sophisticated system, but everyone should have some system because the more records you have, the more claims you can prove—and the more money you will save. If your records are incomplete, you're likely to pay Uncle Sam more than you legally owe.

If you have never filed your taxes before April 15, you're probably not the type of person who will conscientiously maintain daily records. Perhaps you should accept that as a reality—and plan accordingly!

Determine your style of record keeping and weigh the alternatives for yourself. What are the risks of postponing the task? What is the worst possible thing that could happen? What would you do in that situation? Do you need an ongoing system to feel secure? Is it reasonable to design a system that requires daily entries, or is it more realistic to accept the fact that you will not deal with taxes until April?

Crucial Steps
Regardless of your style, there are certain steps that are crucial:

> •If you have a tax advisor, make an appointment to get together well before April 15 to determine exactly what records you need to keep if it is not clear to you. This will eliminate unnecessary paper, and ensure that you retain essential information.
> •Designate a place to keep any information relevant to your tax return. It can be a dresser drawer, a file, a shoebox, a calendar, a computer—in short, anything that works for you.
> •Pay tax-deductible items by check or credit card whenever possible. At the end of the year, sorting canceled checks and credit card receipts is much easier than sorting cash register receipts with blurred dates and miscellaneous unidentified scraps of paper. Some banks and brokerage firms even offer systems that break out taxable items paid by check. Computer software programs are also available for that purpose.
> •Ask yourself how much of your record keeping or tax preparation you really need or want to do yourself. Is there someone who can help—another family member or a professional?

The Ongoing System
In my experience, it's possible — and preferable — to avoid all the last-minute work if you can. What are the advantages of an on-going record keeping system?

A key advantage is that you are less likely to omit legitimate expenses if you record them as they occur. You will also be able to make better financial decisions, particularly if your income varies from month to month, as is the case with many self-employed people.

An ongoing record keeping system also helps in case you're audited. Your chances of defending your deductions are greater if there is evidence that your expenses were noted "contemporaneously," as the IRS states it. Taxpayers are not permitted to re-create records months later to satisfy an audit, unless the records were destroyed in an extreme circumstance such as fire or flood.

If you're audited, records are essential. Legitimate expenses may be disallowed for lack of documentation. If that is not enough to spur you into action, consider the high cost of interest and penalties on past due tax.

Finally, if you've kept accurate records through the year, you'll find it easier to get your information to your tax accountant or file your forms yourself before the April rush. One of my clients routinely used to request an extension on April 15 instead of filing his return. After we worked out a record keeping system, not only did he file his return early for the first time in his life, he received a refund on March 15! Instead of paying a penalty for non-payment of taxes, he received an interest payment on his savings account.

If you choose to keep your records as you go, make an appointment with yourself to get it done, either at the end of each working day, or at the time you pay the bills. If you record expenses on a calendar, choose one with enough space to write—or use a separate notebook. Don't let perfectionism defeat you. If you forget to record a luncheon expense at the time, decide what you can do next time. A less-than-perfect system is still better than no system at all.

Keep accurate records of income from all sources—for example, your job, freelance work, and interest paid and capital gains realized from savings accounts and investments. Note the source of the income in your check register. IRS auditors frequently match deposit records to amounts declared on tax returns. If you cannot prove that a $2,000 deposit is repayment of a loan to a friend by showing a copy of your original check or other transmittal, the IRS could treat the entire amount as taxable income.

File records of deductible items such as medical bills, charitable donations or casualty losses as soon as you get them. The system that demands the least amount of work has two clearly labeled envelopes for each deductible category: expenses paid by check or credit card, and cash receipts. The information in these envelopes should not be needed unless you are audited by the IRS and need additional supporting evidence.

The April Approach

It is also possible (with certain preliminary precautions) to wait until April 15 is just around the corner, and still do the job effectively. It makes little difference whether you spend 10 minutes a day, one hour a week, or three days a year working on taxes. If waiting until the last minute is your normal approach, accept it and plan for it. Here's a game plan that should help you out.

Even if you prefer the April Approach for organizing your records, remember that you still must have the records available when the time comes. First, collect the records—canceled checks, credit card receipts and statements, bank statements, cash register receipts, calendars, and any articles or other information you may have collected about what you can deduct—and sort them.

When all the papers have been separated into the appropriate piles, place each category into a separate container, such as a large envelope, plastic basket, or shoe box. Label each category clearly. Since you will probably need more than one sitting to complete your taxes, these labeled containers make it easier to clear your work area, if necessary, and to find your place when you are ready to continue.

Now, take one category at a time. Eliminate duplicate receipts. For example, keep either the customer copy of a credit card payment or the copy sent with your monthly statement. Always keep the receipt with the most complete information, or staple the receipts together. If you need to correlate your charges with your calendar in order to prove a tax-deductible expense, such as in the case of entertainment, put all receipts in chronological order to speed up the process.

The Electronic Method

Even if you are Almost Paperless™, you may feel more comfortable keeping some paper to prove to Uncle Sam that your records are accurate. But that is changing quickly! This year my tax accountant wants all information I send him in electronic form, so your choice may be determined by the person you use to file your taxes if you don't do it yourself.

If you use your computer for managing your finances, you'll certainly want to consider a software program for preparing returns! TurboTax (www.turbotax.com) is one of the most popular. This web-based program allows you to login and work on your forms anywhere, save your work and return later.

Preparing to File

Whether you keep your papers organized through the year or you wait to organize them when you do your taxes, the rest of the process is the same. If you prefer paper, use a calculator with a tape to total the receipts for each category of deductible items and staple the tape to each pile. Write the category on the tape. Alternatively, you can track them in a computer spreadsheet. If you use an accountant, make an itemized list of your deductions so the accountant can double-check your work, and so it will be easier to support your claim in the case of an audit.

While you've held onto most of the information concerning your deductions through the year, other records of deductions and documents regarding your income will be supplied by others, so watch your mail carefully. Mixed in with the usual junk are documents critical for your tax return.

These include:

- A W-2 form from your employer, if you work for wages;
- A 1098 detailing how much mortgage interest you paid last year;
- 1099 forms, if you are an independent contractor, own stock that paid dividends, or had interest or other types of non-wage income. If you have kept good records, you can match the 1099s against them. This double-check not only helps catch any errors; it also keeps you from overlooking taxable income if the 1099 doesn't show up. If the IRS gets a copy of a 1099 and you don't, their computers will spot the underpayment and audit you for the money plus interest and possible penalties.

Now you are ready to begin entering the information on the tax forms, start an online tax filing program, or take the information to your accountant (many accountants will provide a worksheet for compiling information).

Keep the tax returns themselves forever.

What Should You Keep—and for How Long?

Once you've finished filing your return, the next consideration is how long to keep the material you've collected. The simple answer is to keep whatever you need to persuade the IRS that everything on your return is accurate. Hang on to the evidence for as long as the IRS has the right to question your return.

Ordinarily, that's three years from the due date for the return, including extensions, to assess any additional tax. But, a return can be audited for up to six years if the IRS suspects the taxpayer has neglected to report substantial income. There is no time limit if fraud is suspected.

Your record keeping system doesn't have to be elaborate or sophisticated in order to work. What is more important is to have a system—and the discipline to keep the files up to date.

Set up a separate reference file for each year's tax information, and separate it into folders for each itemized deduction: medical, taxes, interest, etc. Save any bills, receipts and canceled checks that correspond to those deductions.

If you write off the cost of a business car, keep the logbook in which you recorded your trips as well as evidence of the costs you incur.

If you claim someone who is not your child as a dependent, keep a separate file for the evidence that shows you provide more than half of that person's support.

Keep information relating to the purchase of a house at least six years after the sale of the house. This includes your title, deed of purchase, information about your home's purchase price and the cost of major capital improvements.

Records that verify the amount you paid for an investment (your cost basis) should be kept for three years after you've sold the investment and reported your gains or losses on your tax return.

Keep the tax returns themselves forever.

Remember, you may want some records, such as warranties for major purchases, beyond the time the IRS requires for audit purposes.

It May Come As a Surprise...

Most taxpayers don't really have to file by April 15 because they don't owe a dime on their returns! There's no penalty for missing the deadline if you are due a refund. But don't wait too long! You still have to file a return; failing to do so until after the IRS figures you are late—and asks you about it—could mean a penalty.

Chapter Seventeen

Your "To Read" Pile

Whether electronic or paper, your "To Read" pile may be one of your biggest challenges. Most of us find it tough to stay current with all of the newspapers, magazines and books we want to read, especially now that we're also reading emails, blogs and online articles. Add in professional journals and newsletters, instruction guides for all the electronic gadgets we've got in the house, and promotional materials for insurance policies, self-improvement opportunities and political candidates. The task of keeping up with our reading can become overwhelming.

Regardless of whether your reading is online or in paper form, solving the problem of too much reading means accepting the fact that you can't read it all.

We all want to be "well-read" so that we can be well balanced in our knowledge and be more productive. We also feel we should read broadly because we worry we might miss something that could be very important to our lives, or at least be a lot of fun! And we'd like to be well-read to make a good impression on our friends and business colleagues.

There's a very positive aspect to an overflowing "To Read" pile. It shows that we have many interests, which makes us interesting, creative people. Remember that a creative mind always has more ideas than the body can carry out. Many of those ideas come from what we read, but what we must remember is that there's no shortage of resources for ideas. There will always be more things to read, so spend your time reading, not feeling guilty over what you haven't read.

Almost Paperless™
If the paper pile itself is the problem, try moving your reading online. You don't have to own a tablet computer to enjoy online reading. Most newspapers and magazines have online versions. Some newsletters you receive can be sent to your inbox instead of your mailbox. Make a list of the items you receive and spend time

researching whether there is an online option. In many cases, it will also save you money, because the online version is free. (Though that is changing in some cases.)

You might be thinking you have to go to multiple websites to read it all, which would be very tedious, but these days, that's not necessary. All you have to do is create a "reader" for yourself and sign up for subscriptions to the items you want to read. They are called RSS feeds, and if you use a web-based email program such as Gmail or Yahoo, you already have a reader. You can also try NewsFire, Vienna, Newsgator, netvibes, thunderbird, RSSowl or bloglines.

Within your reader, you can click on "add feed," and it will often provide a list of options for you and give you a place to add a specific URL for the blog or newspaper you want to read. To find out what that URL is, go to that newspaper's website and look for the orange RSS button. Copy the URL into your feed reader, and voila! Articles will automatically appear as they are posted. As you scroll through the headlines, you can click on them for the full article/post or skim your way to the bottom. It will automatically mark them as read, and you can choose to save items if you wish.

You can also set up your smartphone to access your reader when you are away from the computer.

Be Selective
Regardless of whether your reading is online or in paper form, solving the problem of too much reading means accepting the fact that you can't read it all. Even if you take the best speed-reading course the country has to offer, the law of rising expectations will undoubtedly prevail: If you increase the speed at which you can read, the amount of information you want to read will also increase.

The issue is not reading faster, but reading smarter. One of the first rules is to be more selective. Do you really need to read every newspaper article in your RSS reader? Can you subscribe to a different RSS feed that just gives you the "top" stories or posts? If you're getting too many emailed newsletters, try unsubscribing from a few. The "unsubscribe" button is usually near the bottom of the message in very small print.

For paper users, instead of taking the time to browse through a magazine or journal, check the table of contents for articles that relate to your specific interest. Read lead paragraphs, lead sentences and closing paragraphs to get the main idea. Beware of the lures of modern day marketing! Do you catch yourself reading a publication or major advertising promotion just because the promoter made it look so appealing, while at the same time ignoring a publication you must read to be current in your field?

*Play a game with yourself to see how much potential reading material
you can eliminate before it ever gets to your "To Read" pile. How much
can go directly into the recycle bin or "marked as read?"*

If you can't resist the temptation to read everything that comes into your house—even if you have no need to read it—take yourself off of mailing and circulation lists.

Also, be particularly leery of those publications you receive as business perks. Ask yourself, "If I were paying for this publication out of my own pocket, would I still order it?" If not, cancel it, or give it to someone who would benefit more from the subscription.

Make an inventory of the magazines and periodicals you receive each month – online and in paper. Estimate the amount of time it would take to read them the way you'd like to. Are your expectations realistic? If not, what can you do about it? Identify which publications contribute the most value. Consider alternating subscriptions every year or two.

A friend of mine was constantly irritated by the pile of daily newspapers that she did not get to over the course of the week. It added stress and a sense of obligation to the point where she felt forced to read a weeks' worth of papers on Saturday, just because she paid for them. The problem was quickly eliminated when she amended her subscription to receive only the weekend papers.

Improve Your Technique

When you have eliminated absolutely everything you think you can, try to improve your reading techniques.

Perfectionism is one stumbling block in reducing the "To Read" pile. For example, you receive an alumni newsletter in the mail. You're interested in the news of your former classmates, but there simply isn't time to read it now. So, you put the newsletter on the credenza behind your desk or in the basket beside your lounge chair in the family room. If it's electronic, it remains in your inbox or in your "To Read" folder. Guess what? Six months later it's still there—along with the next five issues!

Or, you may receive a journal from your professional association. You feel obligated to keep up with the latest happenings and there are some activities in which you would like to participate, but there's no time to read the journal when it arrives. Into the basket/folder it goes. By the time you get around to reading it a month later, the seminar that really suited your needs is full or already over.

The end result in both of these cases is usually that you eventually tire of seeing the clutter, and toss or delete everything.

There are no magic words to make your "To Read" pile disappear if it's too high. You have three options: Read it, file it, or throw it away. If you choose the first option, you face a time-management problem. There is only one way to read, and that is to create the time to do it.

Make an appointment with yourself to read and mark it on your calendar, just as you would make an appointment with someone else to go to the movies. Consider your own biological rhythms. Is it easier to get up an hour earlier or stay up an hour later? Can you take your lunch to work two days a week and read through your lunch hour? To stay abreast with your business reading, can you set aside a "quiet time" each day, or two to three times a week, when your assistant will screen out all but the most important calls? Or, can you put your phone on voice mail?

Incorporate
Look for creative ways to incorporate reading into your daily life. One man I know has started riding the bus to work. The commute is slightly longer, but now he has time to sit and read through his RSS reader each day using his smartphone.

Do you travel frequently? If so, designate a place to put reading materials you can take with you on your next trip. Then, use those inevitable delays as a gift of reading time instead of a total disaster.

Do you drive a carpool for your children and end up waiting for them, spend time waiting in doctor's offices, or go to meetings that frequently begin late? Always carry reading materials with you so you can make the time productive. If you have a smartphone, it's easier to access those articles, and carry them with you.

I'm not suggesting that every uncommitted moment should be spent reading—or doing anything else. Sometimes the best way to use a few unexpected moments is to do some deep breathing or fantasize about a vacation! However, if you carry reading material with you, you can make a conscious choice instead of finding yourself in an unconscious trap. Keep in mind that it can be "fun reading!" One client of mine loves to read spy novels. He always carries one with him on airplanes—the only time he enjoys that relaxation luxury.

Categorize Your Reading

Separate your reading into different types of reading. Keep all high priority reading together so that when you have set aside reading time you won't be tempted by material that belongs in a lower priority category.

Put material from other categories where it can be read as time permits. For example, many people enjoy reading mail-order catalogs when they want to relax. If you do, put a basket beside your bed where you can collect the catalogs, and read them at your leisure. When the basket gets full, that's your signal it's time to toss some out— or start over completely (note on the front cover the page numbers for items of interest).

Another category might be materials that you would like to read, but are not a high priority and will be outdated at a specific time. Jot down on the cover the deadline date for reading. If you haven't read it in six weeks, or when the basket is full, throw the material out! This category of reading is a good one to carry with you when you're traveling. As you finish reading something, you can toss it out, thus offering the added incentive of lightening your luggage!

Put each category of reading in a location where you are most likely to read it. For example, I like to read catalogs when I'm watching television, so I put them in a basket beside my chair. I do "high priority" reading when I travel, so I carry those in a file in my briefcase.

"Just in Time" Reading

My experience has made it clear to me that we are more apt to read immediately those articles that relate to important or timely issues. For example, if you find an article on planning a birthday party for a five-year-old, and your son just turned four, your motivation to read the article will not be very great, but if his birthday is a month away, you will be very interested in the information.

When you find an article that interests you, but you don't have time to read it, tear out the article, file it according to the topic it relates to and discard the magazine. Then, when you are dealing with the topic, it will be much easier to determine if the article is useful. If the article remains in the pile of magazines behind your credenza, it's highly unlikely that you'll remember the article, let alone have the time to go through the pile to find it!

Keep in mind that in today's world, if you save something too long it could easily be out of date by the time you get around to it. And, because there is so much information available online, you can easily find information about almost any topic later. If you feel comfortable with this, you can toss the magazine, and make a note of the topic in your files for later reference and research.

However, if you need to save articles related to your personal or professional interests, consider creating a separate file system that I call a "Library File." To determine where information should go, use the same question you would ask for your reference files: "What word will I think of if I want to find this information?" For example, an article about how to choose a caterer could go in a library file called "Entertaining," or an article on antique restorers could go in "Decorating" or "House Information."

A client of mine who is a physician scans the table of contents of his medical journals as they arrive, notes which articles he wants filed and jots in the margin the name of the file where they should be filed. His assistant then files the articles so they are available for his reading when he is dealing with a particular medical problem.

Always read with a pen in hand. If you find a magazine article you'd like to save but can't tear it out because your spouse hasn't read the issue, or there is another article of interest on the other side, just note the page number of the article (and the subject, if you wish) on the cover. Then, later on, when you're faced with stacks of old magazines, you will be able to identify quickly which contain articles you want to keep. (You may also discover some articles interest you less than they did when you marked them!)

Set Limits

One of the most common questions I get from clients is "How long should I keep books, newspapers and magazines?" There is no right or wrong answer to this question. The answer depends entirely upon your feelings about these publications. For example, some people enjoy being around books, whether they have read them or not—or ever intend to read them. They appreciate books the way other people appreciate art or scenic views. If you feel that way about books and you have enough bookshelf space, then by all means keep them.

However, if you're like me and having too many books creates stress, then eliminate those you've read and don't intend to read again, and those either given to you (even if they did cost a fortune!) or that you picked up off the "Under $2" shelf in the local bookstore and that you never expect to read. But, don't just throw them away! There are many productive uses for unwanted books. As for the books you still want to read, make an appointment with yourself and get to it.

Several years ago I was feeling particularly burdened by my books. I realized that many of them I would never read again, but I was reluctant to get rid of them. "Why?" I asked myself. Suddenly I realized it was because I wanted to remember that I had read them! The solution? A list of books in my filing system with the books I had read, the author, and two or three sentences about the book. Problem solved! And the local library loves the books I donate every year for their annual fundraising book sale!

For online reading, you're best not keeping too much too long. Many blogs and periodicals you subscribe to online will inundate you with dozens of articles daily. The key is to skim for the quality items and pass on the rest. Some days, you just might have to "mark as read" on last week's material and start fresh.

What about magazines and newspapers? Again, there is no right or wrong answer. Look at each publication individually and make a decision about how long you will keep it. For example, if you have young children, you may feel compelled to keep issues of National Geographic as reference material for future school projects. If you really enjoy cooking, or you entertain frequently, you may decide to keep Gourmet permanently. News magazines, however, are of little value when they are more than a week or two old, unless you happen to be a historian or a journalist.

> *Use the Sunday paper as my signal that it's time to discard the previous week's papers.*

If there are articles I really want to read but did not get around to, I tear them from the paper and file them in my reference file as discussed earlier in this chapter.

Identify those items that are of extremely limited value when they become outdated. Last week's TV Guide, old phone books, catalogs from stores from which you've never ordered, and last month's Newsweek are primary candidates for the trash or the recycling bin.

If you really enjoy holding on to publications, what is the best way to do it? The first step is the same one we use in organizing so many things: "Put like objects together." For example, keep all travel books together, all kitchen magazines together, and all catalogs together. If you like, put colored dots on bookbindings to make it easier to keep them in the appropriate category. Put magazines in cardboard or plastic magazine holders, labeled with the name and year of publication. Then, when you see the amount of one category you have accumulated, you can determine whether you really want to take up that much of your living space with that item.

After you've categorized all of your reading material, and eliminated anything that you decide is excess, the final step is to designate a place to keep it. To determine that, ask yourself where you would be most likely to read or otherwise utilize the information. If it is reference material, in what room would you look for it? Travel and foreign language books might be best in the library or family room, while light fare such as People or Reader's Digest might go in a basket beside your lounge chair to read during commercials. Millions of us enjoy reading in the bathroom, so a magazine rack hanging on the back of the bathroom door might be the perfect place for the lightweight reading!

Alternative Measures

If bookshelf space is a problem even after you have eliminated all the publications you can, then what? If you have some books that are important to the family but not particularly to you, identify your alternatives. Is there someone else in the family who would enjoy them more? If your children want the books, but they are not in a position to take them now, put them in boxes in a safe, but less accessible location in your home—clearly labeled!

If you have books that no longer interest you or your family, donate them to a library or professional association, or sell or trade them at a secondhand bookstore. If you have a large number of books, check online to find a book dealer who will pick up the books at your house, so you can avoid the hassle of having to cart them around.

Consider alternatives to reading. There is nothing that says you are un-American if you don't read the daily newspaper (although you'll undoubtedly be more informed if you make a 15- to 30-minute appointment with yourself each day to read one). A friend of mine says it took him years to admit that he really could read all he wanted to of the newspaper by looking over the shoulder of the person standing next to him on the subway! Instead of reading the paper, consider skimming the headlines online for 15 minutes at the start of your day.

Another way to keep up with books that you'd like to read is to buy—or rent or borrow—the audio version. Books on CD are a great way to relax, or to educate yourself while commuting. I regularly listen to these CDs in my car. If you have an mp3 player, you can also subscribe to podcasts the same way you would an RSS feed and download those to listen to on your device. Many of these podcasts are free and updated daily, including NPR's many programs.

A client of mine used to have all kinds of books, magazines and newspapers all over her house until she built a new house and discovered what it cost her per square foot. When she saw what her packrat behavior was costing her, she threw all the reading material out. Remember, this country is full of libraries!

Chapter Eighteen
Your "To Write" Pile

One thing that has changed considerably during the past few years is letter writing. Instead of sitting down at a desk with pen and paper, we send quick emails, or messages on social networks. In many cases, this hasn't made getting those letters written any easier – or gotten it done.

The mobility of our society and our changing lifestyles has created an enormous network of people with whom we would like, or think we ought, to communicate. High divorce and remarriage rates result in larger, extended families. Despite new tools for communicating, these situations have complicated our lives and made it more difficult than ever to keep up written communication.

Personal Correspondence

As with every other aspect of paper/file management that we've discussed, selectivity is the key. There will always be more people to write to than you will have time for, so choose those who mean the most to you. Keep in mind that circumstances change, and we do outgrow friendships. At 22, you probably felt that your college roommate would always be an important person in your life, but your paths led in different directions and you now realize you have little in common.

If you're serious about keeping up with your friends through messages, the most important thing to do is to set aside a regular time to write them, such as one Sunday per month, or one letter before your favorite television program. Write just one email message each week, and you can communicate with 52 friends each year.

Do whatever you can to make writing letters/emails enjoyable and efficient. Some of us would never write to our family and friends if we had to write by hand—and in the case of a few people I know, the recipients wouldn't be able to read the letters if we did. Personally, I love letters—all letters—and I have yet to criticize someone who wrote me an email instead of a letter.

If you're going to write by hand, choose stationery and a pen that you like and find easy to use. Select different styles of writing paper for different occasions. Carry notepaper in your handbag or briefcase so you can jot a quick note while you wait for an appointment. This is also a great way to use postcards that you pick up while on vacation. Sometimes you may find it convenient, or even fun, to take a box of note stationery and your "To Write—Personal" file with you to the doctor's office or the beach.

Thank-you notes and letters of condolence are two especially important kinds of correspondence. Not only do we want to do what is socially correct, but we want people to know we appreciate their kindness, and care about their suffering. In some cases, you may find it's easier for you to make a telephone call than it is to write an email. However, in other cases it is still appropriate to send a hand-written thank-you card. If you feel you must write a message, do whatever you can to simplify the process. I find it helpful to purchase multiple copies of any thank you or sympathy cards I particularly like. If you don't have a card on hand and don't have time to get one, write a note on personal stationery.

We often put off writing a letter because there are so many things we want to say. But, the longer we put it off, the more there is to write. Then we decide we will wait until Christmas, the holidays come and go, and the Christmas cards we managed to purchase are still in the desk drawer. Finally, we are so embarrassed by our negligence that we completely lose contact with a friend.

If you recognize this scenario, ask yourself when was the last time you got a short email or note on Facebook from a friend and complained, "My, that sure was a short note!" A short note is better than no note at all. Beware of perfectionism. Write what you can when you can, and the people who are truly friends will understand and be glad to hear from you.

Birthdays and Anniversaries

There are a variety of ways to handle these annual special events. First, find a place to consistently list birthdays and anniversaries—a special occasion book, part of your calendar, or a section of your "To Do" book.

Next you've got to find a way to remind yourself to look at the list. One person I know checks her list at the beginning of each month and transfers into her calendar the days she needs to mail the cards or gifts (not the day of the birthday, when it is usually too late to take action). You may prefer to put all the reminders into your calendar at once for the entire year. Many electronic calendars can be set to repeat events such as birthdays or meetings each week, month, or year. You can also subscribe to online reminder services. I found quite a few when I entered "birthday reminders" into my favorite search engine.

One of the risks of purchasing greeting cards in advance, even if you don't know to whom you will send them, is forgetting that you have them—or not being able to find them at the right time. To avoid this, establish a specific place to keep the cards. Be sure that it is easily accessible if you want to encourage yourself to use them! If you keep more than 12 or 15 cards on hand, organizing them by occasion will save you time and prevent frustration. Buy one of those beautiful cardboard boxes, or use large 8 1⁄2" x 11" envelopes (tuck in the flap to make a large pocket envelope), and write "Anniversary," "Birthday," etc. on the outside. Arrange the envelopes alphabetically, and put them in your reference file.

Business vs. Pleasure
Separate your "To Write" category into "Business" and "Personal." You may feel in the mood to write a quick thank you note, but not to inquire about a discrepancy in your credit card bill.

If you're using paper, chances are still high that you're typing the business letter on a computer. Make sure to keep plenty of paper and printer ink handy. Another quick way to write a short business letter is to use a personalized postcard. I had some personalized ones printed to use for requesting information or confirming appointments.

My solution for personal and business greeting cards is Send Out Cards. It's quick, cost-effective, and professional. You can try it out for yourself at https://www.sendoutcards.com/papertigerlady/.

Chapter Nineteen

Family Records

A father had to revaccinate his 5-year-old for school because he couldn't find the child's immunization card, and the doctor who treated her was no longer in practice. A business executive missed an important financial opportunity when she needed to fly to Italy, but couldn't find her passport. A financially strapped widow lost more than $2,000 in medical insurance re-imbursements, because she didn't file the claims within the two-year time limit.

Although medical records will eventually go paperless, many of our vital records and documents remain on paper. (See list on page 95.)

What if you need to make an overseas business trip, or you want to sell some stock—could you find your passport or records of the stock purchase easily? What if you or your spouse—or both of you—suddenly died, or became incapacitated? Would someone know where to find your will, or what insurance benefits you have? What about the key to your safe deposit box? Could anyone find the cash stashed away in a money market fund? Make sure that any information your survivors may need is easily accessible.

If any of these questions make you feel uneasy, it is essential that you organize your records. As you do, you will be able to identify areas that need attention, such as out-of-date wills, inadequate homeowner's insurance, missing legal documents, or a beneficiary change you need to make on your insurance policy. Chapter 13 explained how to organize and maintain reference files. This chapter suggests some of what material should go into those folders.

Bank Records
Your files should include the name and address of each bank, credit union, or savings and loan association where you have an account. Also include each type of account, the account numbers and signers on the accounts, as well as the numbers of CDs and the location of passbooks, statements and CDs.

Many banks block joint accounts when they receive notification of death of one of the joint owners. If this is the case, each spouse may wish to set up a separate emergency account in his or her own name. Ask your bank to write you a letter stating its policy, just so you know beforehand.

Credit Cards and Charge Accounts

List account numbers and the names of issuers, so that lost or stolen cards can be promptly reported missing. In the event of death, survivors can notify issuers of the cards and inform banks if accounts are to be closed, or listed in a different name.

Tax Records

Be sure that family members know where to locate information for filing income tax returns, and where you keep records from previous years. Chapter 16 has detailed information on this subject.

Investment Records

While the monetary rewards resulting from investments can create a great sense of security, for many people the paper generated by those investments often creates a great sense of insecurity. One of my clients had a four-drawer filing cabinet filled with annual reports dating back more than a decade. She had never read any of them, but she was convinced she should keep them—just in case!

Investment companies send many different kinds of information. Some can be thrown out immediately; some need to be kept until you've made a decision on the information; some material needs to be kept as long as you keep a particular security. For example, investment companies regularly send out material intended to inform you of their recommendations for stock purchases. If you decide not to buy the stock, you don't need to keep the recommendation. But, if you do act on the information, you'll need to keep the subsequent records of the purchase, along with statements that show how much the investment appreciates or depreciates, so you'll have an accurate record when you eventually sell the stock and have to figure your tax on the transaction.

Keep a separate file for essential information, including your monthly statements and the confirmations of your various transactions, as opposed to the generic information that is sent to all investors. Here's an outline of the kind of information you should have in your files:

Stocks, bonds and mutual funds

Where are the certificates kept? (Safest option: Have your broker hold all your stock certificates.) List the name and address of your broker, and keep a list of holdings, including owner's name, date bought, and purchase price for each security.

Keogh, IRA, 401(k) plans

Some of this can now be maintained online. For each family member, include the name of the institution and the location of papers, if you have some. They may be kept at another location, such as at your office, or with your attorney.

Other investments

For collectibles, what kind do you have? Where are they kept? Who should appraise them for sale or insurance purposes? If you own businesses, what type are they? Where are they located? Where do you keep important documents relating to them (in a safe at the business, or your safe deposit box, for example)? Who should be contacted if there's a problem?

If you own real estate, note who else owns the property if it is held jointly. This includes property owned jointly by married persons. If the joint owner is not a spouse, give the name, address, and interest of each joint owner.

Include the name and address of the mortgagee, how the property is titled, the date of acquisition and cost, mortgage terms (including the original amount), the monthly payment and the payment due date, and the date of final payment.

Retirement Income Records

When planning ahead for retirement, it is extremely important for you and your spouse to have a complete up-to-date record of your pension plan or plans, any annuities you will receive, rents or royalties, and your estimated social security benefits. You can obtain a leaflet called "Estimating Your Social Security Check" from your nearest social security office, and you can obtain a statement of your social security earnings by sending a "Request for Statement of Earnings" form to the Social Security Administration. These forms are available from your local office, or online at the Social Security Administration website.

In most families, one person handles the majority of the financial matters. If you've been the family comptroller, you know the intricacies of the situation. Continuity in planning and implementing financial strategies is important, and while you can't expect someone else to follow your exact track, you want your successor to understand what you have been doing. This means that, in addition to listing where the assets are, you should provide information on managing any complicated situations to help your successor take charge of your affairs.

Trusts

List any trusts you have created or trusts created by others in which you possess any power, beneficial interest or trusteeship. Include the name of the trust, location, trustee and beneficiary.

Wills

For couples, the importance of both parties having up-to-date wills cannot be overemphasized. The individual who makes no will forfeits any assurance that his or her property will be distributed according to his or her wishes, and will probably cause unnecessary difficulties and possible financial losses for the survivors. When a person dies without a will, the distribution of the estate is governed by state laws that may not fit the best interests of the family. (Will-signing savvy: Have an extra witness observe the signing, even more than the law requires. If your will is ever probated, one or more of your witnesses may have moved away or died. Use witnesses you know personally so that they can be easily located.)

Review your will periodically. If you have married, divorced or remarried, if heirs have been born or died, if the size or nature of your estate has changed, or if you have moved to a different state, your will needs to be updated.

Liabilities Records

There are two primary reasons for keeping a complete liabilities record. First, should you become ill and require hospitalization, your family should know not only to whom you owe money, but also when payments are due, to avoid unnecessary complications. Second, should you die, a comprehensive record of your liabilities serves as a basis to dismiss any false claims made against your estate.

Include installment debts on home(s), automobile, credit cards, home improvements, personal loans, furniture, appliances and business loans. Information needed includes current balances, monthly payments, due dates, and whether there is debt insurance.

Insurance Records

The information about your policies is important for two reasons. In the event of your death, it ensures that your family and executor of your estate will know what insurance benefits are available, which companies and insurance agents to contact, and how to file claims. In addition, should you become incapacitated due to accident or illness, your family will be able to pay policy premiums to keep your coverage in force.

Automobile and homeowners insurance policies should be kept in your reference files so you can refer to them quickly to update or check coverage.

Keep life insurance policies in your safe deposit box, but keep information in your files identifying the name of the company for each policy, the policy number, face amount, beneficiaries, whether there has been a loan taken on the policy, premium due date, and the agent's name.

Also keep medical insurance policies in your files because you will need to refer to them when making claims. Some health insurance systems keep track of claims online now, and most are submitted by your doctor's office or hospital directly to the insurance company. You should still retain your copy of receipts for payment and any records. If you do still need to file your own claims, the simplest, most effective way to keep track of their status is to create three file folders. Every insurance claim falls into one of these three stages, so it's simple to check on the status of any claim as it moves through the system.

Label the first "Medical Insurance—To Be Submitted." This contains the blank claim forms, the instructions on how to submit a claim and any receipts from the doctor, laboratory, clinic or pharmacy. Label the second file folder "Medical Insurance—Submitted, But Not Paid." This contains a photocopy of the patient copy of any claims you submitted for reimbursement but for which you have not yet received payment. Finally, the third folder is labeled, "Medical Claims—Paid." This information should be kept for three years to support any medical deductions taken on your tax return.

Medical Records
In addition to insurance records, it is important to keep individual medical records. The simplest method is to establish a separate file for each family member ("Medical—Mary" and "Medical—John," for example). Include doctor and dental receipts that identify diseases and treatments. (These can be culled from the "Health Insurance—Paid" file). Also, note in these files information about blood type, eyeglass prescriptions, and allergies.

Finally, many people like to keep articles about medical developments or pamphlets they pick up at the doctor's office or the pharmacy. Do not include this information in your medical records file. Make a separate file for these informational materials, for example, "Medical Information—Coronary Care."

Survivors' Benefits Records
Tragically, many survivors' benefits are left unclaimed because the survivors are unaware of their existence. These benefits are not paid automatically. Applications must be made on prescribed forms and specific documents must be furnished.

The most well-known benefit is Social Security. Survivors of deceased veterans or active-duty service personnel are also eligible for benefits through the Veterans Administration. These benefits do not conflict with claims made under social security, but again, they are not paid automatically. In most cases, claims must be made within two years following death.

There are several other possible sources of survivors' benefits, including Worker's Compensation, employer's insurance policy, life insurance policy, health/accident policy, auto/casualty insurance, trade unions, and fraternal organizations.

Keep all relevant policies, addresses, phone numbers and contact names in your files, and be sure your family is aware of these benefits, and where the information is filed.

In Case of Ill or Aging Family Members
This is one of the most difficult areas of paper management, but it's also one of the most important. Make sure your own records are in order and that someone knows where you keep them. In addition, be sure you or another family member possesses or has access to the information for any family members for whom you or they are responsible.

You will need a Power of Attorney if that person dies or becomes unable to make his or her own decisions. In addition to dealing with matters necessary in the event of death, changes in records also need to be made for automobile titles, stocks and bonds, bank accounts, etc.

Here's one more very important thing to consider: Be sure to include any special instructions to the family about your memorial service, funeral, or burial preferences. It will be a big comfort. A friend of mine said she felt guilty when her mother died because she did not know whether she wanted her wedding ring left on when she was buried.

Family History Records
The purpose of this category is to assemble in one place important family information that might be necessary to obtain a passport, apply for Social Security and veterans' benefits, or to file a loan application. For each family member, include birth date (a copy of birth certificate if available; original should be in safe deposit box), Social Security number, and a copy of marriage or divorce certificate. Any family genealogy records can also be kept here.

Include in this file the names and telephone numbers for your accountant, financial planner, employee-benefits advisor, insurance agents (life, health, car, personal property, homeowners), stockbroker, or other financial advisor.

Education, Employment and Military Records
Keep a separate file for each family member. For example, "Education Records—Paul" and "Military Records—Bob." The information in these files simplifies the task of writing or rewriting a resume, applying for admission to an educational institution, or applying for a new job.

Household Inventory
One of the most neglected family records is the household inventory. If there is a fire or burglary in your home, this record will help you remember what has to be replaced and to determine the value of each item. An inventory is also an excellent way to

make certain that your insurance protection is sufficient. One client of mine purchased a $15,000 painting but neglected to add it to his insurance policy. When someone accidentally damaged the painting, the owner had to pay for repairs himself.

When you make an inventory, start at one point in the room and go all the way around, listing everything. The more complete the information, the more valuable it will be. Include information such as initial cost, model numbers, brand names, and descriptions. Take photographs of the room and special items so that identifying or replacing them will be easier. Videos make excellent inventories. Be sure to include the basement, garage and attic. Estimate the replacement cost for each item, and add up the total to determine how much insurance you should have. As you take inventory, mark your property with some sort of identification. Your police department may have a special identification program. You can also purchase engravers to mark items with a code you think up.

Update your inventory every six months or so by adding recent purchases and adjusting replacement costs. Some insurance policies automatically increase replacement costs. Be sure you know the limits in your homeowner's policy with regard to valuables such as jewelry, furs and art.

If you find the task of preparing a household inventory overwhelming, check online or in the yellow pages to find a professional to do it, or get other members of the family to help you. Keep the records in a fireproof safe at home or in your safe deposit box.

Warranties and Instructions
The kitchen gadget has become both the joy and the frustration of the modern American kitchen. It is a joy when you can find it when you need it, but it's a major frustration when you can't remember how to operate it, or you can't find the instruction book!

Every time you purchase a new appliance, toy, tool, or other household item, you are blessed with several new pieces of paper: a consumer registration card; a promotion brochure for other products from the same manufacturer; an instruction booklet; and, frequently, a consumer questionnaire. To further complicate matters, often a company will issue the same warranty for several products. Just because you can find a warranty doesn't mean you will know what it protects!

There are several steps you can take to minimize this problem:

Decide whether you will keep all of the information. You may want to throw out the questionnaire, and many instruction books can now be found online. Then, decide where you will keep the information you want to save.

I don't recommend separating them because often one piece of paper will have the warranty and the instruction. You may decide to keep those related to kitchen appliances in the kitchen so they will be readily available, or if your kitchen storage space is limited, you may choose to put them in the household reference file under "Warranties and Instructions." It's also helpful to put the instruction booklet with the stereo, telephone or tape recorder so you can refer to it easily. Keep instructions relating to clothing (if they are not attached) in a plastic bag in the laundry room. Write the name of the item—such as "blue comforter"—on the instructions.

Keep the receipt with the warranty.

Whenever you make a purchase, staple the receipt to the warranty information so you can easily prove date of purchase, or put the date on the front of the warranty for your own information.

Decide now whether you will or will not fill out consumer information cards and warranty registration cards.

We often take longer shuffling the card than it would take to fill it out! The manufacturer doesn't require that you complete the cards to make the warranty valid, but it is essential if you need to be reached for product recall.

Safe Deposit Box
Keep papers that are difficult or impossible to replace in a safe deposit box or a fireproof box in your home. The box should be large enough to hold everything that should be in it—and small enough to keep out things that do not need to be there. The box should not be used as a catchall for souvenirs.

Keep a list of everything you have in your safe deposit box in your reference file at home, and update the list as you add or remove items. If you store documents from investment properties or securities, the rental can be claimed as a deduction on your tax return.

Finally, make sure family members know where the box is located, and where the key is kept.

Emergency Documents Kit
It's a good idea to keep an easy-to-grab, re-sealable plastic bag or container in case you have to leave your home quickly in an emergency. Contents could include:

- Traveler's checks and cash, including change for phone calls in case your cell phone is lost or damaged
- A list of banks and other financial institutions you use
- A videotape of everything of value in your home

- Photocopies of deeds to property—or any records that would be difficult to replace
- Copies of important medical and eyeglass/contact lens information.

In Case of Death...

You may not like to think about such things, but by planning ahead some of the stress involved when a family member dies can be limited. Here are some lists of information someone in the family should have, or have access to.

To get a burial permit, you will need:

- Name, home address, telephone number
- How long in state
- Occupation and title
- Name, address and phone number of business
- Social Security number
- Armed services serial number
- Date and place of birth
- Citizenship
- Father's name and birthplace
- Mother's name and birthplace

You will also need these documents:

- Deeds to property, automobile titles
- Insurance policies
- Income tax returns
- Military discharge papers
- Disability claims
- Birth Certificate or other legal proof of age
- Citizenship papers, if naturalized
- Will
- Social Security card
- Death certificate (certificates for burial permit)
- Bank books
- Marriage and divorce certificates, if any

You will need to notify:

- Doctor or health maintenance organization
- Funeral director or memorial society
- Institution to which remains may be donated if living will exists
- Memorial park
- Relatives, friends, employers of deceased

- Insurance agents
- Attorney, accountant or executor of estate
- Religious, fraternal, civic, or veterans' groups
- Newspaper regarding death notices

What to Keep in Your Safe Deposit Box

- Adoption papers
- Automobile titles
- Birth certificates
- Citizenship papers
- Copies of wills (original, in most cases, should be kept with County Registrar of Wills)
- Death certificates
- Divorce decrees
- Household inventory and originals of pictures (include appraisals and receipts)
- Important contracts
- Leases
- Life insurance policies
- List of insurance policy names and numbers
- Marriage certificate
- Military records
- Passports
- Patents and copyrights
- Property deed and other mortgage papers
- Retirement plans
- Stock and bond certificates and notes

Give serious consideration to the value of storing vital information in such a way that other members who need to access it in case of an emergency can find it. My personal solution is PBWorks. For more information, go to www.BarbaraHemphill.com.

Chapter Twenty
Memorabilia and Photographs

It's September. The summer vacations, family gatherings and neighborhood barbecues were great fun. All that remain are warm memories – along with 657 digital photos on your camera's memory cards, and 13 hours of digital video.

Of course, none of this is organized so that you can actually show it to someone. Add today's new digital content to the boxes of old, unidentified family photographs your mother passed on to you for safekeeping, the trunk of family memorabilia you married along with your spouse, and the piles of creative clutter your children produce. There seems to be no relief in sight.

Feelings, Feelings
Emotional involvement is the trickiest part of managing photographs and memorabilia. Even if we have no real interest in them, we feel that we should have some interest because they represent our family history. How do you know what your heritage will be while you are living it? We feel burdened because the memorabilia was so important to our parents, or because it might be important to our yet unborn grandchildren. In the meantime, what do we do with all the stuff? It fills our attics and basements with boxes, our computers with Gigabytes, and our minds with guilt.

There are several steps you can take. First, recognize that is there no right or wrong approach. To decide what you want to do, begin gathering information about the alternatives you may have. Determine who else might be involved in the decision-making process.

It's impossible to foresee exactly how your descendants will feel about this information. You can only make your decisions based on your current conditions and resources.

It Only Seems Hopeless
When you consider the amount of love, time and money that have gone into your memorabilia thus far, you feel obligated to do something. The question is, "What?"

The simple baby books and photo albums like those our mothers used are no longer adequate for most families. Your intentions are good, but the mechanics of the task seem overwhelming—and even if you have the motivation, where do you find the time? How do you begin? What if you don't have the motivation? Can you risk ignoring the issue? And what about the space that all this memorabilia takes up in your house that you could be using for something else?

The most important step in dealing with the situation is to recognize that if left unchecked, it is only going to get worse. As life goes on, the memorabilia simply accumulates. If the old stuff is out of control, just think what another year's worth will be like!

Instead of wasting energy berating yourself every time you open the closet door and see those boxes of old photos, decide what action you can take to stop the cycle, and then do it. As with so many other aspects of paper management, the best way to make progress on this seemingly impossible task is to start with material you collect from today on. For the time being, ignore those piles of yesterday's memories. You can work on the backlog after you have devised a system that works for you.

A Sensible Solution
One of my clients had a particularly difficult time dealing with her photographs. Keeping up with them was a continual frustration. She decided to come up with a system to correct it—one that fit her needs and circumstances—and that is exactly what she did.

She began by deciding not to bring photographs home until she had taken certain steps at her office, where she had her film photos developed. First, she threw away any photographs that she did not like for whatever reason. Even if you don't print your photos, these principles still apply with digital. Immediately delete any photos that are blurry, show off your right thumb, or that you simply don't like.

Next, since she was printing images, she dated the photos. (Note: Don't write directly on printed photos—write first on an adhesive label, which you can then apply to the back of the picture.) She didn't allow this step to become overwhelming, causing her to procrastinate about the project altogether! She made a commitment to herself that the date is the only absolute requirement. (I would add names to that, so years from now you'll know who's in the picture.)

(Note: If you are saving your photos on a computer instead, be sure to rename them from "DSC00057" to dates with names or places.)

Then, she prepared a pile of heavy envelopes addressed to her parents and her in-laws. Her photo-processing store charges very little for duplicate prints, so she can order them automatically and send selected duplicates to the relatives. This is even easier with digital cameras, because you don't have to keep track of the negatives. You can order a CD and mail that to those who don't want prints, or use it to upload photos to social networking sites, or email them directly to friends and family. There are also many photo-sharing sites out there, such as Shutterfly (www.shutterfly.com) and Picasa (http://picasa.google.com), enabling you to upload photos for your friends and family to view, download and print.

Finally, she put the remaining printed photographs into the plastic pages the photo-processing store gave her when she paid for the pictures. All she has to do when she gets home is put the pages into a loose-leaf notebook.

An extra bonus resulting from her solution is that other members of her family have become much more interested in the photos, because they are easily visible instead of buried in boxes in the closet!

She has since applied similar systems to other paper problems with success. She didn't think she had the discipline to do it, but she did. And you can too.

Start with today's digital photos and find a system that works for you. Maybe you fill up one memory card before emptying it into your computer and sorting through them. Maybe you cap yourself at a certain number of photos. Either way, it's best to have some sort of trigger that says, "Time to take care of this."

As with so many other aspects of paper management, the best way to make progress on the seemingly impossible task of photos is to start with material you collect from today on.

When saving photos in your computer, one system that works for many people is to create a folder for each year. Within the "2011" folder, there can be folders for certain months. This way you can save miscellaneous pictures. You can also create folders for specific trips or events within that year. As long as you give them a name you will remember, you can always use that name to do a search later – even if you can't recall what year you went to Disney World.

Computers have the added bonus of enabling you to view your photos in a slideshow format. Set your laptop on the coffee table, hit "play," and show off your trip to Fiji to your guests. For the more tech-savvy, you can even hook your computer up to your TV for better viewing. This requires a special cable with multiple holes in it, usually an HDMI cable. Check with a knowledgeable friend, your IT department at work, or the local electronics store.

Caution: Just like any digital data, be sure to back up your photo files into "the cloud" as discussed in Chapter 6. That external hard drive will not help you if your house, computer and it all go up in flames.

Another Approach

A friend of mine has a beautiful antique trunk in her family room. It is filled with photographs—labeled with names and dates—but in no particular order. She sits on the floor with her grandchildren and shares her "treasure chest of memories." It is of no concern to her that the photos may be in less than perfect condition for future generations. She wants to enjoy them now!

Make It Easy on Yourself

You've got to recognize that you probably won't have the time to organize family memorabilia as perfectly as you'd like. Determine what you're willing and able to do, and do it.

As my client did with her photographs, design a system to fit your particular needs. Start by identifying an accessible place where you will put all the memorabilia as you receive it or find it.

If you have a small amount, two boxes labeled "Photographs" and "Memorabilia" (napkins, brochures, invitations, matchbooks, dried flowers, etc.) may be all you'll need. If you have difficulty putting things away in their proper place, leave the lids off the boxes so they will be easier for you to use. At the end of the year, put the lids on the boxes, clearly label them (for example, "Photos—2002"), and put them away.

If you are short on storage space, put your boxes in an out-of-the-way location, such as the attic or basement. (Be careful not to store the boxes near a heat source or where it's moist. You don't want to go through all the time and trouble of storing valued memories only to find them ruined.) You can make a note of where they are on your reference-file index.

Take whatever steps you can to make the organization process easier. If you don't have time to go through and label each picture, make a note on the outside of the photo envelope as to the major categories, "Summer—2001," or "Jerry's Birthday Party—2006," for example.

Some cameras will date the photos for you, and if you're having prints made, the lab can add dates to the back of your photos. (In the lab though, remember, the date indicates when the film is developed, not when you took the pictures. Put a date on any memorabilia such as travel brochures, napkins, etc. as you receive it.

You will be able to re-create the occasion much more easily if you decide to organize the materials in a more sophisticated style.

If you are a "memoraholic," you may need to divide your treasures into smaller categories to make them more manageable. There are several ways to do that. For example, if you have more than one child you may wish to have a photo album or memorabilia box for each one. Or you may want to create categories by type such as "Children's Art," "Playbills," "Trips." These can be further broken down by destination and date, such as "Europe—1999."

Get Kids Involved

If you have children who are old enough to be involved in the decision making, ask them how they feel about the issue. You can give family memorabilia to your children, but be sure to do so with "no strings attached." Let them decide what to do with it based on their own needs and perspectives. If you feel strongly about what should happen to a particular keepsake and you would be hurt if your children didn't follow your wishes, keep it yourself.

Perhaps you've got material that's not important to you or your children. Ask a professional buyer of memorabilia if what you've got has any particular value to other people. If it does, perhaps you can give it to a charity, or sell it to a collector.

If you or your children feel it's important to go through everything yourselves to determine what you should keep, you'll need to develop a system for doing that. When time is a major factor, you may find it necessary or desirable to hire a professional organizing consultant to help you. If your children think it should be done, get a commitment from them as to how and when they will help.

Going It Alone

So, you're going to fly solo through this project? Then you'll need a plan for accomplishing the task. Will you have to do it in bits and pieces, or is it possible to spend several days working on the project? In either case, set goals for yourself. When you are having guests for dinner after work you can fix dinner in an hour if you need to, but if you have all day Saturday you can spend hours preparing dinner. This project works the same way. The more time you allow, the more it will take.

If your home has plenty of storage space, your decisions about what to keep may be different from someone who lives in a small apartment.

If you're having trouble parting with some items but don't have enough space, try to find ways of using memorabilia in your home or office. Thanks to the help of a creative friend, I now enjoy decorating with many memorabilia treasures formerly buried in drawers, taking up space and never seen or enjoyed.

The Knack of Good Photo-Albuming

After you have taken all, or even some, of the steps described thus far, don't be surprised if one day you discover you really are ready to get those old prints into albums. It's a terrific project for when you're housebound for one reason or another. If you usually save your photos electronically, you still might want to create a special scrapbook or album for a particular event or trip. If you're not inclined to do so yourself, you can hire someone to help you with this.

If you are taking on this project, take whatever steps you can to get into the right frame of mind. Look at the process as a wonderful adventure into memory land. Get into comfortable clothes, put on your favorite music, fix a pot of coffee (but don't put it where you risk ruining any photographs if it spills!), and you're on your way! Take the following steps:

1. Choose a good place to work.
Work in a comfortable chair at a large, clean, flat surface in an area where there's plenty of light and where you can leave the project until it is completed—or at least long enough to make some major progress. Resist the urge to rush out and buy photo albums at this point! Time will give you a better idea of the kind and quantity you need.

2. Sort through the photos.
Eliminate all those unsuccessful shots. Don't be discouraged—even professional photographers use only a small percentage of the photos they take. The first candidates for the wastebasket are double exposures and those fascinating shots of the inside of your lens cap! Very close behind are pictures you wish had been double exposures—like the one that shows only the lower half of your body—and those shots you wonder why you took (the one of the Christmas tree after you took down the decorations).

3. Give away photos you won't use.
Many photos have little meaning to you, but could be special to someone else. They are fun to drop in the mail, and you'll undoubtedly bring a smile to Aunt Amanda's face!

4. Identify the negatives.
Before you separate the pictures from their negatives, write a description on the outside of the packet, such as "Graduation—John, 1997," or simply use dates, and put the negatives in the packet. You may decide that once you have the picture and as many copies as you want you can throw the negatives away. If you want an

"insurance policy" against unexpected disasters such as theft, fire or other loss (or divorce), keep the negatives in a separate place. Perhaps you could exchange negatives with a family member—or put negatives of favorite shots in your safe deposit box.

5. Identify the photos.
Determine whether you are going to put the information about the photo on the back of the photo, or on a separate piece of paper so that it can be read after the photos are in albums. (Some energetic people do both!). The more information you know, the more joy the photo will bring in the years to come—who, what, where, when, and why. Experience has proven that, while a picture may be worth a thousand words, an unidentified picture is worth little to future generations. (Again, don't write directly on the backs of a photo—write first on an adhesive label, which you can then apply to the picture.)

6. Categorize the photos.
Sort photos into the categories you plan to use in the albums. Most people sort chronologically, but some do it by subject matter—for example, "Family Reunions." CAUTION: Label the piles as you work. If you are interrupted it won't take long to proceed with the sorting once you return. One easy way to do this is to purchase inexpensive small baskets that can be labeled temporarily with removable labels or sticky notes.

7. Select albums.
Now it's time to decide what kind of albums you wish to use. A loose-leaf photograph album has a distinct advantage if you are trying to arrange photos chronologically because it's easy to add a page if you find more photos after you finish the project. (Make sure to use albums made of acid-free paper and polyester-based plastic if you want them available for future generations.)

If you want to limit the number of albums you'll need, you may prefer the kind in which the photos are in individual sleeves, overlapping one another. The disadvantage of this type is that it will not accommodate over-sized photos.

8. Into the album they go.
Let your creativity loose! Enjoy experimenting with different arrangements. Feel free to trim photos to their best advantage. If you have several photos from one event, group them together on one or more pages and write a short scenario about the occasion, rather than labeling each photo individually.

Creative Memories consultants offer classes in their homes or yours as well as tools and techniques you can use to create beautiful albums, which will preserve your photographs and other memorabilia. Call 800–468–9335 or go to www.creativememories.com to get the name of a consultant in your area.

Slides, Films and Tapes

Not many people still make slides, but there is a good chance you have a box sitting around – either yours or those from a relative. Label slides in pen directly on the cardboard frame. Write so that you can look at the slide with the naked eye and read the label at the same time. This will be a big advantage should you ever want to put together a slide show.

Many photographers and developers now offer digitizing services, taking old slides and photo prints and putting them onto a DVD for you.

Movies and videotapes should be organized, too. The key is to label them clearly. Keep peel-off labels and a felt-tipped pen in the same drawer or shelf as you keep your photographic equipment. Label as you go—even if you don't have time to do it perfectly.

Be Creative

As you browse through your photos, consider ways of using your favorites in some unusual way. Check with your local photographic-supply or film-processing shop for ideas. Here are some possibilities:

•Make your own note cards or picture postcards. - Paste photos on plain note stationery slightly larger than your photo. "Photo Talk" stickers are available from a photographic supply store, or can be ordered online. You can use the stickers to add amusing comments above people's heads.

•Make a photo T-shirt. - Take a color print to a copy shop that has a heat-transfer machine. Have a transfer made and applied to a T-shirt, or take the transfer home and apply it yourself, as you would an iron-on patch.

- Make a jigsaw puzzle. Available online. A great gift idea!
- Make a poster.
- Turn your pictures into artwork to hang in your family room or college dorm room. Consider panoramic views of places that are special to you. The same companies that make jigsaw puzzles can do this for you.
- Make a calendar. - Custom photo-finishing labs are equipped to print a photo above a 12-month calendar or you can find multiple online services. This makes a great holiday gift idea for children, grandparents, friends or business associates.
- Make a mousepad – Look at your favorite photo every time you use your computer.
- Make a slideshow from slides or photos. This is very easy with digital photos, and you can find multiple online programs to do so. If you have

basic photo editing software, that program may also have a slideshow creator. Some photography stores will also help you do this.

The next time a grandparent or other elderly family member is celebrating a birthday or other special occasion and you can't think of a suitable present, ask if they have any old photographs. Chances are they will, and nothing would please them more than to have your help in putting them in albums.

My grandmother talked for years about all the photographs she had never labeled. She was concerned that she couldn't remember everything about the pictures and that her handwriting was not good enough for future generations. I invited her to tell me about the photos while I made notes. Eventually I found at least one picture of every member in both grandparents' families. Whenever anyone comes to visit, it takes her only a few minutes to find the photo album, and the reminiscing begins. It's still not clear who received the greatest gift.

Keep Those Cards and Letters Coming

Okay, what do you do about all those beautiful greeting cards you've received for birthdays, anniversaries and other special events? What about all the handwritten letters from relatives and friends? If you keep them, you may feel guilty because they take up so much room, and if you toss them you may feel guilty because you care about the people who sent them, or you think they're too pretty to throw away.

There is nothing wrong with keeping every card and letter you ever received, if you have plenty of space to store them and you enjoy looking at them—or just entertain the possibility that you might someday! If, however, you feel a knot in your stomach every time you see them or you don't have a place to put the stationery you need for answering today's mail, then you would be wise to reconsider your actions.

One viable solution for letters is to select the ones that contain information that would be of particular interest in the future. I enjoy saving the letters from my mother that describe special family events, for example.

The method you use for keeping cards and letters will be determined by the way you plan to use them. If you are keeping them strictly for casual reading in the years to come, a box labeled "Letters to Save" will do nicely. If, however, you want to be able to refer to them you should keep them accessible. Try filing them alphabetically in an accordion-type file with alphabet dividers.

I put all the cards I receive for a particular occasion on the mantle in the family room. After two or three weeks, I keep only those that are particularly special—and in some cases I throw them all away because I know there are others, and I am optimistic enough to believe there will be more! A friend of mine keeps all of hers and then every few years makes a collage of them to hang as a decoration. Another friend frames cards she finds particularly beautiful. Some community groups collect them to use in self-help projects for handicapped persons and senior citizens. Sometimes schools are happy to have them for art projects. (See "Recycling" in Chapter 8.)

Whatever you decide to do with them, remember that the sender intended that card or letter to bring joy, not stress—so enjoy!

Chapter Twenty One

The Kitchen Piles

Throughout this book I talk about going Almost Paperless™, with the caveat that even those who get rid of most paper sources still have plenty to deal with — in addition to email and electronic documents.

And where does that remaining paper gather? In the kitchen – the "heart" of many homes. The kitchen counter or table becomes a catchall for a multitude of paper—the newspaper that you left on the table when you hurried off to work or a morning school carpool; the school papers your kids brought home and dumped on the counter; the mail you grabbed out of the mailbox as you raced in the door (now sorted in several unidentified piles!); and the notes, phone messages and recipes that are piled on any available surface. How can you sort all this out?

Kitchen Catch-All
First, create a gathering place to put all the paper when you don't have time to put it away. You could use a large basket, a shelf or a tray. The key to successful kitchen-paper management is to make an appointment with yourself to get back to the pile before it becomes too overwhelming, separating what should come out of the catch-all from what really belongs in the kitchen. You may find it helpful to do it on a regular basis—before your favorite television show, or once a month when you pay bills or, at a minimum, when the container gets full!

Keep the catch-all pile as small as possible by putting things away whenever you can. For example, if as you pick up the mail you see several pieces of "junk mail," throw them away immediately. It will also be much easier to keep the papers in the kitchen at a minimum if you have specific places for papers to go—unread newspapers under the family-room coffee table; newspapers you've already read on the floor in the front hall closet, or in the garage to be saved for a community recycling program, or thrown out.

If your work center is in the kitchen, put the papers you need to act on into your "To Sort" tray until you are ready to take action. If your work center is in another room, take your papers there. Put the papers that belong to other family members in places designated for their attention. Make sure it's easy for the person who is sorting the mail as well as for the people who need to get the mail.

One fantastic solution for managing kitchen paper is SwiftFile, which enables you to sort papers by the date they require action. You can learn more about the SwiftFile Solution at www.switfile.com.

Message Mania

One maddening result of our telephone world is a myriad of notes taken as we talk—or plan to talk—on the phone. What can you do to avoid, or at least minimize, this problem? How many times a week do you find a piece of paper with notes from several different telephone conversations?

The first question is, "Where do I put it?" If you still keep (and regularly use) a landline, place a small notepad by the phone—I like 5" x 7"—and try to use one piece of paper for each call. When the conversation is over, ask yourself, "What is the next action required on this piece of paper?" The answer will tell you where to put it. (See Chapter 13 for more details on this process.) Often, all you need to do is double-check to see that the number is in your telephone-number system, and then you can throw away one more piece of paper.

Designate a system for checking the answering machine if you use one. If your daughter comes home from school, does she listen to the messages? What does she do with those that are not for her? You might set up separate "mail boxes" for each member of your household. You can also use the "memo" capability so that if another family member wants to leave a message they can talk into the machine or the phone, and it will record their message as if it were a regular incoming message.

If you still take paper messages for each other, use a bulletin board, a plastic message holder, magnets on the refrigerator, or envelopes attached to the wall or a door. Be sure the owner's names are clearly labeled so there's no confusion! Encourage family members to note on the message the date and time they took the call.

Returning phone calls can be a big stumbling block. All the organization in the world won't make the phone-related papers go away. Only you, or someone to whom you delegate, can do that.

We talked earlier about your "call" file. If you don't use one, find one place to put all the papers that require calls. Or make a list of the people you need to call (and their phone numbers) and throw out the individual notes. Then, when you have time to make one phone call, it won't require much more time or effort to make two or three.

Kitchen Transitions

Obviously, some papers belong in the kitchen: recipes, cookbooks, entertainment records, coupons (if you are a user and not just a collector), and take-out menus.

Your attitude toward the kitchen, and toward cooking, will determine to a great extent how your kitchen should be organized. There are many factors that contribute to our feelings, and it is important to acknowledge that these feelings change with time and circumstances. This doesn't mean we're lazy or negligent, just that our priorities have changed.

I have clients who are overwhelmed with guilt by the piles of "kitchen papers" because they're afraid to admit that they aren't as interested in cooking as they once were. In fact, I'm a good example. When I was newly married, my husband and I entertained often. We also had three children, and a limited budget. Therefore, I spent a considerable amount of time with papers in the kitchen—collecting coupons, selecting recipes, keeping records of what I served guests, educating myself about the nutritional needs of my children, and reading the food columns in the newspapers.

Later, I was divorced and my children were with me only part time. I ate out often and devoted the energy previously spent in the kitchen on my career. Then, I married a man with two children.

With five teenagers in and out of our home, the organization needs in the kitchen changed dramatically. Because so many family members—and their friends—were in and out so frequently, it became important to have lots of food possibilities at a moment's notice.

I again got interested in recipes, but very different ones from those of 15 years before. For example, I used to believe that if I didn't spend at least an hour preparing the evening meal, no compliment was justified. At this point, I began to look for 10-minute recipes that would generate smiles—or at least fill stomachs! I became much more conscious of the nutritional value of what we ate, and most of my cooking was done in the microwave. Entertaining was much more informal, so soufflés that had to be eaten the moment they came out of the oven were of little interest. Dishes that could be prepared in advance of the event became essential.

Once I understood that my circumstances had changed, I went through all my old recipes, and the recipes I had intended to try. If a recipe didn't fit my time requirements or the dish wouldn't be healthy, I threw it out—at least most of them!

Now, my children are grown and out of our home. My husband and I eat out frequently, so once again my patterns are changing.

Designing Your Cookbook and Recipe System
Let's take a look at the issue of recipes and cookbooks. First of all, accept the fact that you may not organize your recipes and cookbooks the same way that your mother did. It doesn't mean you're wrong—just different, because your lifestyle, priorities and needs are different from those of your mother. So, erase from your mind all of those "shoulds" and think about what you need to make a system work for you.

Almost Paperless™ in the Kitchen
Many 20-somethings I know who are cooking for themselves own very few cookbooks, and have only a few family recipes written down. This is because they can access any recipe online in just a few seconds. There are even smartphone applications that will tell you what you can cook with the ingredients in your cupboard and refrigerator. You can now write your recipes into computer documents, making it easier to search for them later. If you're sick of the paper clutter and feel comfortable using your laptop in the kitchen (placed somewhere out of spill range), then you can reduce the number of cookbooks and paper recipes you keep.

Use It or Lose It
If you think about it, you'll probably find that most of your cooking is done from less than 20 percent of your recipes. I've observed that the axiom "less is more" is especially true in the kitchen. The more recipes people have, the fewer they use. And we often spend more time agonizing over the fact we don't use them—or chastising ourselves because we haven't organized them—than we do cooking them! The only solution is to put a stop to this negative cycle.

If you have many recipes written down and you want to keep them, don't wait to set up a system for today's recipes until you've conquered the backlog. It will be easier to set up a system for the recipes you are collecting now. Then incorporate the backlog into the new system as you pull out an old recipe, or as you have the time, energy and interest.

There are dozens of systems on the market for organizing recipes. If you find one that suits your needs, by all means use it. Personally, I have found that many of them do not allow for the flexibility essential to creating a system that is workable for particular situations. For example, the categories may not be the same as you would use, or the space provided to write, type, or glue the recipe isn't large enough.

This is not a place to let your perfectionism get in the way of starting the task! The system doesn't need to be perfect, and probably won't be. You can always make adjustments as you experiment.

One of the easiest ways to get started is with file folders so you can sort your recipes into categories. Designate a place, preferably in or near the kitchen, where you will keep recipes. Put all the supplies you will need there: file folders, a felt tip pen to label the files, scissors, tape, index cards, recipe cards, a blank recipe book, or whatever system you plan to use.

Your Recipe Categories
There are dozens of ways to categorize recipes—if you doubt it, just compare cookbook indexes—so don't worry about what categories you want to use. Instead of trying to think up the categories first, start with the recipes you have. Ask yourself, "If I were looking for this recipe, what would I think of?"

As a general rule, start with broader categories first, such as "Bread." Then if the quantity of recipes in that category becomes too bulky to manage, you can subdivide it into "Yeast Breads," "Muffins," "Sweet Breads," etc. If you spend a great deal of time cooking or entertaining, and enjoy spending time planning menus, testing new recipes, etc., then you may want your categories to be very specific from the start.

I find it helpful to separate the "tried and true" recipes from those I would like to try. When I'm convinced a recipe is a "winner"—and I don't keep them unless they are—I put it on a 4" x 6" index card and into a card box. The box is divided into categories the same way I divided the recipes in the manila file folders. (A loose-leaf notebook also works well.)

The recipes that I would like to try stay in the file folders. It is not necessary to type or handwrite the recipe unless you particularly want to. The fastest way is to literally "cut and paste" the recipe to fit on the index card. You may wish to make notes on the card about when you served it, to whom, what you served with it, or suggestions for adaptations of the recipe.

Decide whether to separate your microwave recipes from your conventional recipes. Many conventional recipes can be adapted for the microwave, but many people think of them quite separately.

The Recipe Search
If you are routinely frustrated because you can't find a recipe from one of your many cookbooks that was successful on a previous occasion, put a note that includes the

recipe name, cookbook title, and page number in the appropriate category in your recipe file.

One simple solution is to mark cookbook pages with sticky notes. Another option is to create a separate notebook divided into the same categories you use for organizing your recipes. Whenever you find a recipe you like in a cookbook, enter the name of the recipe with the name and page number of the cookbook where you found it into the notebook.

Conquering the Recipe Backlog

Once you have a recipe system set up and working, you can decide whether you want to tackle the backlog. You may decide it makes more sense to toss the entire collection. If you want to incorporate your existing recipes into your system, set aside enough time to do it. How much time you'll need depends on how much you have, what you think about the project, your working style and your circumstances. Will you enjoy the project and want to spend a long time on it, or will you regard it as a frustrating one for which you will have only a limited attention span? Do circumstances dictate that it be done on a piecemeal basis, even though you would prefer to spend more time on it?

Once you have made that decision, write down the commitment to yourself on your calendar. Is there a family member or friend who will help you? If so, get them involved in making the appointment, so you'll be less likely to ignore it. If organizing the recipes is a major problem for you, hire a professional organizer—"Yes, Virginia, there are people who are good enough, and like it enough, to get paid for organizing recipes."

After you've decided when you're going to conquer the backlog, determine where you will actually do it. If at all possible, find a spot you can use until the project is completed. (I declared the dining room off limits to the family for two weeks and did it there.) Or, set up a card table in the corner of a room. It will be much easier, and less frustrating, if you don't have to get everything out each time you want to work—and you may find that you will work a few minutes here and there, unplanned, if everything is accessible. With your cell phone, you can talk to a friend and organize recipes at the same time.

The next step is to collect all the recipes you have—or just some of them if looking at them all at once is too overwhelming—and get organized. Undoubtedly along the way you will feel discouraged and overwhelmed. Keep asking yourself: Do I really need this recipe? Does it exist somewhere else? How long has it been since I've used, or had, the recipe? What's the worst possible thing that would happen if I tossed it? As you sort, you may well discover that your standards change as you begin to realize how much work is involved in keeping everything you had originally planned to keep.

Trying New Recipes

One of the essential steps in keeping the recipes under control is developing a method for trying new ones. Whenever I feel like I'm in a cooking rut, or if I have some extra time, I choose six to eight recipes I would like to try in the next few weeks. Usually I pick one or two main dishes, one or two salads or vegetables, one or two soups, and one or two desserts.

When you've selected the recipes you want to try, take the time to note on your shopping list the ingredients you will need to prepare these dishes. (Obviously, any perishable items can't be purchased too far in advance.) Then clip the recipes to a magnet on the refrigerator or put them in a special compartment in your recipe box or book. When you are rushed to get dinner on the table but want to try something new you will already have the menu idea and the ingredients right at your fingertips. (The same technique can be used in choosing recipes that your children can prepare if they cook while you are working.)

The final step in this system is making a decision about the recipe after you have eaten the results. Was it great? If not, why keep it? Avoid the "I really should give it one more try" syndrome. There are thousands more recipes you can try that might be great, so let it go! Then, your recipe collection becomes something you really treasure instead of tolerate.

One winter, I was snowbound for four days, and I had a wonderful time experimenting with my new recipes. In addition, I ended up with a freezer full of food that could be microwaved for a speedy nutritious meal on the days following the snow when I was too busy catching up on lost time to spend any time cooking.

Entertainment Records

One of my clients had invited a certain gentleman to her home on several occasions with various different dinner guests. She was most embarrassed to discover that she had served tomatoes stuffed with spinach on each of the last three occasions! (Unfortunately, he didn't like it the first time!)

One way to avoid that problem is to create a notebook or computer document to record your entertaining. Just as with the recipes, there are numerous ways to organize this notebook. If you entertain lavishly, and frequently have the same guests, it will require more time to maintain the system than if you entertain simply and/or infrequently. The easiest way is to list the events in chronological order. Include the menu, table decorations, guest list (and seating arrangement, if you wish), and perhaps even what you wore. It is also helpful to list suggestions you may have on any improvements you want to make when you entertain again, whether it is a slight change to a recipe (which should be noted on your recipe card or in your recipe book), a suggestion about serving logistics (for example, that the coffee should be on a separate table or to put out small forks with the appetizers), or a note about the flowers.

If you entertain frequently and are particularly concerned about not duplicating menus for the same guests, you could put a separate alphabetical section in your book. Each guest would have a small section where you could put the date when you entertained him/her. Then, you could check the chronological list for the menu that guest was served. For example, under "A," you would have: "Adams, John—3/6/99; 10/2/10; 5/4/11; etc. You could also note there any items of concern when entertaining that guest—allergies, food preferences, medical concerns, etc.

To Market, To Market

It's tough to keep track of the food we have on hand and the food that we need to purchase. I find it helpful to have a shopping list posted on the refrigerator, along with a pencil permanently attached with a string.

There are paper-management techniques you can use to simplify your shopping trips. If you do the majority of your shopping in the same store, create a checklist of the items you most frequently purchase, arranged in the order of the grocery store aisles. Be sure to leave space in each section for special items that are not regularly on the list.

Either keep it in your smartphone or print a dozen copies. After you've tried it that many times, you will probably find ways you want to change the form. You may want to post the form on the refrigerator door to check off items as you go. However, if there are family members who are unable or unwilling to use the list, it might be easier to transfer the ad hoc list from the refrigerator onto the form just before you go to the store.

If you have problems with people forgetting to put items on the list when they use the last of something, try making a list of commonly used items. Then, just before you do a major shopping, you can make a quick check to see which of those items are in low supply.

Coupon Coordination

A discussion of "kitchen papers" wouldn't be complete without including coupons. Decision-making and organization—in that order—are the keys to saving money with manufacturers' coupons and refund offers.

The first decision to make is whether you are really serious or committed to the idea of coupon clipping. My personal opinion is that unless you enjoy doing it, or your budget requires it, coupon saving is too much trouble. Ask yourself, "Do I really save money when I consider the time it takes me? Do I end up buying more expensive products that I wouldn't necessarily buy if I didn't have the coupon? Is clipping coupons an attempt to assuage my guilty feelings over excessive spending habits, or an effort to appease my mother?" One man I know looks at coupon clipping as a game and uses it for relaxation.

Many people clip coupons only for those products they routinely buy, such as coffee, laundry soap and paper products. Other people spend two to three hours a week clipping and can save $30–$50 per week on grocery purchases, in addition to the amount received in cash from rebate offers. I once read in a newspaper about one woman who bought $113.05 worth of groceries for $1.69. The real price: Her office is a corner of her basement, where she has organized coupons, labels and proofs of purchase into 14 grocery bags, six cardboard boxes, eight filing-cabinet drawers and a bookcase!

The basic principle of organizing, "put like things together," certainly applies to coupons. Establish categories for your coupons in the same way you establish categories for your recipes. Ask yourself, "What category would I think of if I wanted this coupon?"

There are several possibilities for categories, such as "Paper Products," "Cleaning Products," and "Vegetables" (this could be broken down in "Vegetables—Frozen," and "Vegetables—Fresh"). You may want a separate system for refunds, which could be located in the same container but in a separate section. Within that system, you would have the same categories as you had for coupons. In addition, you might want a section for "Refunds in Progress."

Keep a supply of return-address labels, envelopes and stamps on hand. For a refund offer that requires several proof-of-purchase labels, put the labels in a pre-addressed envelope that has the refund expiration date on the top right-hand corner.

The technique you use for storing coupons is also important. Decide whether you will always carry all your coupons with you when you go to the store or whether you will have a "Master Coupon Box" at home from which you can pull out those coupons you want to take with you. While at the store, you can use a regular business-sized envelope (or several) or you can purchase a "Coupon Billfold" designed specifically for that purpose. It is unlikely that the categories in a pre-designed system will be the same as yours, so feel free to put on your own labels to make the system work for you. However you choose to keep the coupons, make sure to purge expired coupons on a regular basis.

> *One woman I know divides her coupons according to the shopping aisles in her local store. Not only does the system add continuity to her coupon and refund hobby, it saves her an incredible amount of time.*

There is no right or wrong decision on this issue. Experiment until you find a method that works for you. Remember, you can change your decision at any time based on your current circumstances. Once your decision is made, concentrate on setting up the system needed to make the decision workable. But above all, create a system that gives you a feeling of success!

One Final Fridge Note

Communication can be a constant frustration in families, particularly in homes where there is a single parent or where both parents are working. To improve the situation, designate a communication center that is convenient for everyone. The refrigerator is usually a good place to put chore reminders. Be sure your messages aren't always things to do. You can also communicate nonessential, but very important messages, such as "Hope you had a good day at school. I love you, Mom."

Chapter Twenty Two

Children and Paper

Children and paper go hand-in-hand in our society. As soon as a couple even begins to think about starting a family, the paper begins to accumulate—information on childbirth classes, ads from child-care services, notices of "mother's day out" programs, descriptions of child-rearing techniques, articles on overcoming fertility problems, and books about the psychological impact of parenting and the "how to's" of surviving parenthood.

These days, a couple is more likely than not to receive much of that information via email or find it online. But what about the stuff that just shows up in the mail, or the brochures you get from the doctor's office? Soon enough, you're dealing with health records, finger paintings and school papers.

There are numerous approaches to surviving this paper blizzard, but the first and most important step (as with any paper-management issue) is to set up some kind of system. As your children grow older, the system will need to change, but you don't need to worry about that now.

For the Parent-to-Be
The first step toward establishing a system that will work for you is to examine your own feelings about keeping and using information. Is it important to you to have easy access to articles about child rearing or would you be more likely to search online, ask your doctor, or discuss it with your parents or a friend? Do you need the information near you to feel secure, even if you never use it? Does having paper around create additional stress, guilt or frustration? Is it realistic that you will take the time and effort required to maintain an extensive library, or is there someone else in the family who will help you?

These are important questions to answer in order to prevent setting unrealistic standards for yourself. You create a "no-win" situation if you feel guilty because you keep too much, and feel guilty if you don't! Eliminate the "shoulds," and acknowledge what will work for you.

Organizing Paper @Home: What to Toss
and How to Find the Rest

Collect and Categorize

The simplest way to begin any system is to collect all the information you have into the largest general category. In this case, that's "Children." You'll probably need both a computer file and a container to keep the paperless and paper items under control. For the paper, find a container, a basket, shelf or file and label it clearly. On the computer, create a folder where you will keep any information you receive. If you tend to bookmark online articles, tag or label them accordingly.

When there is more information than can be easily handled and the file becomes too bulky, divide the information into the next logical categories. For example, information about children can be categorized into areas of concern such as education, medical, memorabilia, legal information, and toys and equipment. Notice that "toys and equipment" are put together; it is often too difficult to differentiate between the categories. However, you may have "Toys and Equipment—Owned" and "Toys and Equipment—Shopping Information."

Our needs are constantly changing. A system that works when a child is six months old might be totally inappropriate when she is sixteen, and the system that works when she is sixteen will be overkill when she is twenty.

For example, when your child is in elementary school, a file labeled "Susan—Education" may be sufficient. However, when she enters high school that category may be too general. The categories you will need at this point depend on your particular style and on your child's interests. If you are very active in your child's educational program, you may need a file for "PTA," "College Preparation," or "Extracurricular Activities." (That last category might need to be subdivided into "Gymnastics," "Scouts," etc.) And when your child has gone off to college, many of these files will no longer be necessary. At this point all the report cards for kindergarten through high school become highly irrelevant. Choose one or two for your grandchildren to see. If you want to keep all the files about your child together in one place, put the child's name at the beginning of each label: "Susan—Education," "Susan—Sports," for example.

If you know that you will not take the time to develop a detailed filing system, find a basket, shelf or file and label it "John—Education." It may take you 10 minutes to go through the entire box if you need a copy of an award certificate to go with a college application, but it will be a massive improvement over having all the members of the family turning the house upside down looking for that large brown envelope!

Teach Your Children Well

With all of the obligations and options in today's world, it is very easy for a parent to spend an inordinate amount of time being a social secretary, or just a "nagger." Teaching your child organizational skills will benefit you and your child—for life!

Our needs are constantly changing. A system that works when a child is six months old might be totally inappropriate when she is sixteen, and the system that works when she is sixteen will be overkill when she is twenty.

One of the biggest problems we all face is making choices. Over and over I find houses buried in paper because adults feel compelled to do it all—read every book, newspaper and magazine, keep every photo and memento, or go to every concert, seminar and reception. Living a happy and healthy life (or even just getting by) in today's world means making choices. Remember, clutter is just postponed decisions. As parents we should teach that concept to our children, and one place to begin is with paper.

There are many steps you can take to help your children learn how to manage the paper in their lives, as well as how to become good time managers.

As soon as your child goes into an organized playgroup or educational program, you will begin to accumulate paper. Designate a special place for her to put the papers she brings home from school. If you start this habit early, you will avoid many panic situations of trying to find a trip permission slip when you should be getting ready for work, or running out the door to catch the carpool. Each evening, or first thing in the morning, you can check and see what came home from school and what requires your attention.

The Art Gallery
It's always a challenge to cope with your child's creative work. Young children can produce enough paper to fill a small art gallery within a week. Which of those 400 finger-painted gems will become cherished examples of the early works of future Picassos?

There's nothing wrong with keeping everything that children create if we have plenty of space to keep it, and plenty of energy to organize it, but few people have either. It's easy to get caught in the trap of feeling guilty if we throw away the things our children make, and feeling overwhelmed if we don't. It is essential to involve your children in the selection process from the beginning.

You can use this process as a tool for teaching them decision-making techniques, which will be important for them to have as they grow up. In my experience, one of the major problems that adults have with organization of their papers—and often their lives—stems from their belief that, if they just got organized, they could have everything and do everything. Not true!

All the papers you'd like to keep can be put in a basket, or on a bulletin board with your child's name prominently displayed. Then when the basket gets full or the bulletin board gets crowded, encourage Susan to choose her three favorite papers, which can be put in a Memorabilia Box for safekeeping. Put the child's name, age, and date on the back of the artwork to make it more meaningful 20 years from now.

There are other creative uses for artwork. Put several creations together and make a collage for your child's wall or to use as a present for a relative. Grandparents, aunts and uncles are delighted to receive letters from children. Have your child write a short message on the back of the painting, or just send the painting—signed, of course! Teach your child the value of recycling. Artwork makes wonderful wrapping paper for gifts—especially for admiring grandparents!

Kids and Calendars
Once your children reach a certain age there are many other steps you can take to help them learn how to manage their paper and to improve their time-management skills. For example, put a large calendar with plenty of writing space in an easily accessible place. The refrigerator is a good choice, because everyone ends up there sooner or later!

Have each child note when he or she needs transportation to soccer, cookies for a school party, or plans to spend the night at a friend's house. This method helps you plan your schedule and avoids last-minute crises. If Sam comes running to you at the last minute and says, "Mom, I need a ride to gymnastics," you can say, "I didn't see it on the calendar, Sam, and I can't take you right now." If he misses an important practice or is late for his game, it won't take him long to realize that he has to take some responsibility for his own life. Of course, you have to take into account unusual circumstances and make exceptions when you feel it is appropriate to do so.

Don't forget that you owe the same courtesy to your children. For the career parent, this is a great place to communicate facts about your schedule that will affect your child(ren). Include travel schedules, night meetings or houseguests. Consider using different colored pens for each member of the family, and attach the pens with a long string next to the calendar so you won't hear the excuse "I couldn't find a pencil!"

As soon as Johnny begins getting school assignments in advance, help him choose an assignment book. Teach him how to plot out complicated assignments by reading one-half chapter each day—or if it works better to read two chapters at a time, choose those days on which there are not other obligations such as piano lessons or soccer practice. Discuss the concept of choosing a style. Remind him to watch for family commitments that might affect his schedule. Recognize that his style may not be the same as yours, but that doesn't mean it's wrong.

Encourage your children to use a calendar to keep track of sports events, babysitting commitments, job responsibilities at home, birthdays they want to remember, etc.

The calendar is also an excellent place to help your child understand the importance of goal setting. If, for example, Susan really wants to take a trip this summer that you feel is too expensive (or you feel she should contribute to the cost) help her plan how she could make it happen by using the calendar. Count the number of weeks until she needs the money and determine how much she will have to make every week if she is to succeed. She can use the calendar to block out time when she will work and set goals for raising the money.

Your Child's Own Files

As your child gets older, help him organize the papers he needs to cope with daily life. Purchase several file folders and help label them according to his needs. Make a category for each subject at school and each area of interest. At the end of the year encourage and assist your child, if necessary, in cleaning out the file and determining what papers he would like to keep as mementos, and which have served their purpose and can be thrown away.

If your children are involved in several organizations, a file called "Directories" can be very useful to keep the lists of participant's names that you receive from scouts, sports, school, youth group, etc. This file can save many hassles when Saturday morning rolls around and you are madly trying to find a ride to soccer for your child. The information is also helpful if your child is sending out party invitations or trying to locate a friend's phone number or address.

One day when he was 15, my son stopped in my office and noticed an X-Rack on my desk (it's a plastic frame designed to hold hanging file folders). He's a "gadget lover" and interested in art. He asked if I would get him one. The combination of the uniqueness of the file holder and the brightly-colored file folders with plastic tabs fascinated him—and gave me a terrific opening to help him set up a file system for his needs. It is very important to do whatever you can to make the organizing process appeal to your child. It's a great way to create one-on-one time, and you benefit doubly because both of your lives will run more smoothly.

Your child may also want files that relate to special interests. For example, your teenager might want a category on "Fashion" or "Shopping Ideas" to take on her next shopping trip.

Be sure your child makes a file index or list of the files to keep in the very front of the files. For an example of one 19-year-old's file categories, see the list at the end of this chapter. Of course, our children are much more apt to keep things on a computer and may not need as many files. Again, the idea is to create a system that works for them and suits their needs. If your children prefer paperless, encourage this behavior but make sure they learn the principles of organization within those files. Teach them that even if you have two terabytes of space, you still don't need to keep everything. And of course, make sure everything is backed up in the cloud as previously discussed.

You'll See Results Later

Caveat: Just because you teach your children how to organize doesn't mean you'll see the results! However, it has been my experience that as they get older and see the benefits to organization, they will begin to practice what you've taught them.

A 19-Year-Old's File Index

- Car

- Carnegie Mellon—general

- Carnegie Mellon—courses, grades, loan

- Employment—paycheck stuff, rules

- Finance—bank account, student loan applications

- Hobbies

- Legal stuff—leases/credit card info

- Medical

- Resume

- Stories

- Taxes

- Utilities

- Video games

- Writing/papers

Chapter Twenty Three

Travel and Paper

Travel is a good example of how technology is slowly (slowly) inching us toward an Almost Paperless™ society.

Yesterday, you needed papers for airline bonus programs, car rentals and hotel rooms. You had maps, directions, confirmations, tickets, itineraries, notes about people to see and things to do, papers you needed to take with you on the trip, addresses and phone numbers and traveler's checks.

Then there were all the papers you collected while you were traveling: more maps, phone numbers and addresses of new friends made, favorite restaurants and shops, receipts for purchases that are being shipped to you, boarding passes and ticket stubs, travel brochures and a variety of memorabilia. If your trip involved any meetings, you'll undoubtedly have a pile of papers that contain all kinds of wonderful information you want to keep or use.

Today, this is changing. You book your hotel online and receive a confirmation via email. Same with the plane ticket, and your airline now might use paperless boarding passes and keep track of your bonus miles online. Your smartphone has a GPS in it, so you don't need maps or directions. You use a debit card instead of traveler's checks, you have a phone app that will suggest great places to eat, and your itinerary is stored in a spreadsheet or as part of your calendar – all accessed from your smartphone or computer.

Yesterday, you arrived home from the trip with the best of intentions about going through all those papers, but as soon as you walked in the door you were confronted with all the mail that arrived while you were away. So the trip papers were pushed aside and eventually ended up in a drawer somewhere, never to be seen again.

Even with all our technology today, you might still walk in the door and have the same problem. Why? It goes back to the basic principles of organization. You might have it all in your phone or computer, but it's scattered all over. Maybe you kept it all, forgot to practice the Art of Wastebasketry® while you were away, and now have no desire to go through those files. Even if you're tech-savvy, you probably still have some papers to deal with, such as receipts to give to your boss for reimbursement.

So, let's take a look at the various areas and see what can be done to manage the travel-related papers and files in our lives.

Essential Information

First of all, consider the travel information you want to keep for reference. This would include maps, travel brochures, information from past trips, newsletters from travel services and information on bonus programs. The first step is to get all the information together. You may have a lot of this still on paper.

Next, think about whether this information is still useful. Is it recent? If it's on paper and you rely on your smartphone, will you really take it with you on your next trip? Can you find that information somewhere else?

Take the items you want to keep and put them in a file or a box labeled "Travel Information." Or, if you're dealing with computer files or online documents, create a folder in your system for travel.

If you travel extensively, you need to decide how to organize the information. One way would be to group it by category. Make a pile or file for maps, another for airline information, another for travel brochures, etc. These could then be incorporated into your reference file under "Travel," so the labels would look like this: "Travel—Airline Information," "Travel—Brochures," "Travel—Receipts," etc.

You might also find it helpful to put frequent-flyer information in your contact list, along with the phone numbers of the airlines.

If you use a frequent-flyer program and receive paper statements, you will soon discover that your airline files become bulky very quickly, so it is important to establish your retention guidelines. I would suggest you keep your monthly mileage statements for as long as you participate in the program, because sometimes airlines offer special bonuses to travelers who have accumulated a certain number of miles during a certain length of time.

Most airlines send out a monthly newsletter. Whether you receive this electronically or via snail mail, keep only the latest one, unless there is specific information that you need in an older newsletter. If so, mark clearly what information interests you so that you can quickly identify why you kept that particular newsletter.

This same system will work for hotel and car-rental bonus programs. Of course, the most important information to have is your membership number.

"Tie-in Programs" are another of the complicating factors in this issue. For example, certain airlines have reciprocal privileges. Or, if you fly one airline and rent your car from a tie-in agency, you can get bonus miles. There are several books and newsletters on the market that describe these offers. If you're serious about collecting bonus points, one of them might be worth your investment.

Maps and Brochures
Maps can be another paper problem for the traveler. If you use a computer and a GPS unit, you may feel comfortable getting rid of U.S. maps. If you travel to a certain country regularly, it might be useful to keep that map, but if you go only once every several years, your version might be out of date by your next trip.

Some people just enjoy keeping maps. If you have only a dozen or so, one file or box will be plenty, but if you have more than that, refine your system by geographic area. I started with "U.S.—Northeast," "U.S.—Northwest," "U.S.—Southeast," "U.S.—Southwest."

What about travel brochures? To determine how these should be filed, you need to identify why you are keeping them at all. The answer might not be the same for each brochure. You may be keeping one strictly as a memento of a beautiful experience, another as a reference in case you return, or another to share with a friend. Ask yourself, "Under what circumstances would I want this information?" The answer will help you determine where you should file it. Put a date on the brochure when you file it, so it will be easier to clean out the files in the years to come.

If you have more than eight to 10 travel files for paper items, I suggest you create a separate filing system—say, a separate drawer—for travel, rather than incorporating them into your existing files. Identify travel files with a particular color so you can recognize them easily.

I used to have voluminous travel files, and now I have very few, and by the end of the year, expect to have none. It's so easy to find information in the Internet from anyplace at any time that I find it's not worth the space, time, energy, or money to save!

Before the Trip
As soon as you begin planning for any trip, make a file with the destination on the label, such as "New York." This will provide an immediate place to put any information regarding the trip—tickets, itinerary, reminders of things you want to take

with you, contacts you want to make while you are there, or places you want to visit or shop. You may have several trip files at one time. One woman I know does this with computer files. Each file contains several items – one spreadsheet for her trip budget, another for her itinerary and various Word documents for checklists and other notes.

> *If you travel frequently, make a standard packing list. Keep it in your "To Do" Book or in your suitcase. Then, as soon as you begin planning a trip, take the list and put it in the destination file. As you think of things you want to take with you, note them on the packing list.*

When you pack your suitcase, check off each item and note the specific number taken. For example, "Dress Shirts—6." (One client puts her list in a plastic folder and uses a grease pencil to check it off. Then it can be easily erased after each use.) If you are concerned about losing your luggage and being able to substantiate a claim, keep the list until after you return from the trip.

People who travel with children can use the list to help their children get everything repacked in the suitcase. When my daughter was twelve, she decided to take the list with her so that when she was repacking her suitcase, she could check it off to be sure she remembered to bring everything home with her.

Make a "Pre-trip Checklist" to remind you of last-minute tasks that are easy to forget, such as "Check thermostat," "Turn off coffeepot," "Stop newspaper," or "Arrange for plant and pet care."

If you've filed your travel reference material by geographical area, it will be very easy to check that file for any additional information you might want on a particular trip. Sometimes I even take the file with me for airplane reading. Be sure to take your list of frequent flyer numbers. These could be listed in your cell phone or in your "To Do" Book.

On the Trip
If you are going to attend any kind of meeting while you're on the trip and will be collecting a number of papers, I suggest you create action files for the trip. It will be easier to make decisions about what you want to do with the papers and files as you acquire them than it will be to go back through the papers when you return home. These action files might include "Write," "File," "Pending." (See Chapter 11.)

What about travel receipts? You can't decide what to do with a receipt unless you know why it is useful to you. Do you need it to prove a tax deductible expense? If so, it could go with other tax information for the year. (See Chapter 16.) Are you keeping it until the china that you purchased arrives safely? If so, it could go in a "Pending" file. When the china arrives, the receipt could go in a "Personal Property" file in case you need it to substantiate an insurance claim.

After the Trip
When the trip is over, put your ticket stubs and boarding passes in the airline file until you are certain your miles have been credited to your account, then throw the boarding passes away. File the ticket stub only if you need it for a specific reason—for example, a business reimbursement or a tax deductible expense. Otherwise, throw it away.

Take action on any papers or files you have brought home with you (or saved to your computer), or incorporate them into your existing action files.

Finally, be sure to purge the trip file itself. Throw away any information that is no longer relevant and file the remaining information in the appropriate place. Suppose, for example, you meet someone on a trip who lives in another city you visit frequently, or hope to visit one day. Put her name and address with a note about where you met in that geographical file. If you save your contact list in your phone, you can create categories for certain people and perhaps place her information in that category. Does all this sound like too much drudgery? It may be a lifesaver if you find yourself stranded in her city one day, or just a lot of fun if you get together and reminisce about all the fun you had on that Caribbean cruise!

For the Frequent Traveler
If you participate in several frequent flyer programs, you'll need a separate file for each airline, so you would have a series of files such as "Airlines—American," "Airlines—United," "Airlines—Delta," etc. If you're horrified at the thought of so many files, consider this: Suppose you're rushing out of the door to grab a flight, and the last thing you need to do is go through a pile of papers from an airline you're not taking. It will take only a second to grab the information from the appropriate airline file – or find the right one among your computer files.

Family Fun
If you enjoy taking day trips but have difficulty deciding where to go on the spur of the moment, create a "Day Trip Ideas" file. Information in the file can also help when you have house guests. "Vacation Ideas" can also be a useful file when it is time to decide on a summer vacation plan.

Chapter Twenty Four
"Paperholics"

There is nothing wrong with keeping every greeting card and letter you've ever received, if you have plenty of space and it brings you pleasure. If, however, your daily living is impeded because of papers out of the past, you need to examine your actions.

While for most of us paper management is something we can live with, for others it is an insurmountable struggle. Their daily lives are seriously hampered, and in some cases brought to a standstill, by the endless clutter of unfinished projects, unread newspapers, magazines and books, unanswered mail and unfiled paper in unidentified piles, bags, and boxes throughout the house. I call these people "paperholics."

Each individual may feel his or her situation is unique, but thousands of people experience the same distress. For some, this constant stress can lead to physical ailments. Some paperholics live in fear of being discovered and go to great lengths to avoid having friends and relatives come to their homes. Some even close off parts of their houses. Others cover up their embarrassment with humorous signs like "A clean desk is a sign of a sick mind," or "Enter at your own risk!"

Many paperholics end up paying unnecessary service charges and tax penalties or having their household utilities cut off because they couldn't find or complete the paperwork. Paperholics constantly make excuses for their behavior or deny it entirely. Some rarely go anywhere because they cannot enjoy themselves until their paperwork is finished. Others never stay at home to avoid facing the chaos. Marriage and family relationships suffer seriously when the paperholic's clutter intrudes on others.

Who Are the Paperholics?
At the end of virtually every presentation I give, at least one person, and often many people, share stories of the people they know, and love, who suffer from this problem. They come from all walks of life, and often appear totally together in their

professional lives. Paperholics can be people of any age. A paperholic is someone to whom every piece of paper represents an opportunity, an obligation, a threat, a memory or a dream. Paperholics keep piles of articles in case they need to prove a position on a particular issue. They hold on to newspapers because they haven't had time to read or clip the articles. (The irony is that usually they cannot find the articles when they want them, and sometimes they don't even realize that they have them.)

There is nothing wrong with keeping every greeting card and letter you've ever received, if you have plenty of space and it brings you pleasure. If, however, your daily living is impeded because of papers out of the past, you need to examine your actions. The reason and degree of attachment, and the ability to let go due to new circumstances distinguishes between normal and pathological saving. Psychologists have studied people referred to as "packrats." They believe that, for some, the problem is a result of an early childhood trauma—a significant loss of some kind. For many people, the problem got out of control because of extenuating circumstances such as ill health, renovating or moving, family crisis, loss of job, etc. All the causes of this behavior are not clearly identified, but most savers are not pathological hoarders.

People who have the most difficulty managing paper are often the people who generate the most paper. They feel compelled to make duplicate copies so they will be sure to find at least one. Many order information booklets from every available source—even on subjects that may not relate to their lives. They tend to take advantage of every offer for a free magazine issue, fully intending to cancel the subscription later. They take copious notes on any available piece of paper.

They pick up information brochures and articles wherever they go. They often subscribe to more magazines and newspapers than they could ever possibly read—and end up reading few, if any of them.

In the end, paperholics live in a vicious cycle. The more paper they accumulate, the less able they are to manage it, and the more out of control they feel.

If You Are a Paperholic
It's essential that you admit you have a problem. Recognize that change does not happen instantaneously. Shelves overflowing with books and outdated magazines, boxes of paper and paper-shuffling habits accumulated over years won't disappear overnight. Behavior patterns take time to unlearn and relearn. Paper-management skills do not come naturally to everyone.

One of the most frequently asked questions that professional organizers hear is, "Why is it so difficult for me to let go of all this stuff?" The answer is not a simple one. Not much formal study has been given to the problem, although it is one from which many suffer.

Accept the fact that you cannot undo what you may feel are mistakes. Take the advice in this book with the idea of starting over with today's papers. Ignore the backlog for now. Create a place to work that you find pleasant. Set up your paper-management center (as described in Chapter 3) to handle today's paper.

Keep asking yourself the question, "What is the worst possible thing that would happen if I didn't have this piece of paper?" Begin to imagine how you will feel when you are successful. What will your house look like? What things will you do that you aren't doing now?

Even if you read all the guidelines in this book, if you are a true paperholic it is unlikely that you will be able make the dramatic changes you want to make without assistance of some kind. It is essential to find people you trust to help you. Here are several possibilities:

Consider finding a self-help support group in your area. Two excellent organizations that offer newsletters, publications, and information about support groups are:

Messies Anonymous
www.messies.com
5025 S.W. 114th Avenue
Miami, FL 33165

***

ICD - Institute for Challenging Disorganization
http://www.challengingdisorganization.com
1693 S. Hanley Road
St. Louis, MO 63144
314.416.2236

You should also consider seeing a mental-health professional to help you deal with such psychological issues as why you need to hang on to all that paper.

An organizing consultant can work with you to go through the paper piece by piece.

You might also find a very special nonjudgmental friend or relative who will work with you or encourage and support you. (I must add that such a person is often not easy to find.)

Of course, a combination of any or all of the above may be necessary.

Paperholics

If Someone You Love Is a Paperholic

If someone you know or love is a paperholic, you may be asking "What can I do?" Truthfully, maybe nothing. It's easy for us to be critical of others who find it difficult to do what we do easily, and it's important to accept that correcting the situation will require much more than just applying self-discipline.

Sometimes letting a paperholic know that other people have similar difficulties can be a great relief. One of the most common reactions to the scenarios I present in paper-management seminars is, "When did you see my house?"

Perhaps the most important lesson I have learned about living with a paperholic is the importance of defining boundaries. If possible, negotiate with that person regarding what papers (magazines, newspapers, photos, etc.) are acceptable in shared spaces. Identify other areas of your home where he or she can accumulate paper according to his or her own wishes. When the papers begin to spill into other areas, you will have the right to take steps to correct the problem. Communication is a key issue. Often it takes time and practice, as well as professional assistance, to master effective techniques.

Finally, acknowledge that all of us have issues we need to resolve. Concentrate on your own issues and allow the paperholic to solve his or her own problem.

Real Life Paperholics

• An internationally recognized medical researcher asked me to help organize his office. When I arrived, we literally rolled piles of paper out of his office on his chair to make room for me to stand!

• A woman called and told me she hadn't had anyone in her home for more than ten years. The reason? Paper piled on every flat surface, stuffed in shopping bags under the bed and shoved in all available drawer and cupboard space. Her children tried to help, but every attempt turned into an emotional disaster. The situation came to a head when the condominium management called the fire department.

• An elementary school teacher wrote that his entire house, as well as his work area at school, was filled with paper. The thought of throwing anything away made him physically ill.

• One woman told me she had moved out of her apartment and into a new one. Not unusual, except that she kept the old one for the purpose of storing all of her paper!

• A client slept on the sofa in his living room because the twin beds in his bedroom were covered with the papers he had accumulated after his wife died.

• Another client had files full of vacation ideas but he had not left the city for more than two days in more than ten years.

Chapter Twenty Five

Caging That Tiger

At this point, a review of the basic components of this paper-management system is in order. Keep in mind that every piece of paper or electronic file in your life can be categorized and put into one of "The Magic 6™."

- Desktop Trays
- Wastebasket/Recycle/Shred
- Calendar
- Contact Management
- Action files
- Reference files

Every time you find a pile of papers or group of computer documents that require decisions, ask yourself these questions about each piece:

- "Can this be recycled/shredded/deleted/trashed?"
- If not, "Do I need to make an appointment with myself to do something?" If so, enter the information in your calendar.
- "Does this piece of paper require action or recall by me at some yet-undetermined time in the future?" If so, enter it in your "To Do" list.
- "Are there any addresses, telephone numbers, or pieces of 'mini information' that I should put on my contact list?"
- If you entered the information in any of the above places, "Do I still need to keep the piece of paper/electronic document?" If so, "Does this piece of paper/document require action or am I keeping it for reference?"
- If it requires action, "What specific action do I need to take?" The answer will tell you into which Action File you should put it.
- If I am keeping it for reference, "What word would I think of if I wanted this item again?" The answer will tell you into what Reference File you should put it.

Getting Rid of the Boxes

In the question and answer period following one of my speeches, a woman asked, "I have four large packing boxes full of papers that I have been telling myself for three years I will organize "one of these days,' but each time I try I am totally overwhelmed. What can I do?"

I told her that I could think of only two options for getting rid of the boxes: Decide that since she survived for three years without any of the information in them she could take a deep breath and toss them all in the trash; or go through the papers one by one using the system described in this book, making decisions on each piece of paper.

You have the same choices for dealing with your accumulated papers and files. It may help you determine which option you want to choose to know that going through the equivalent of one vertical-file cabinet drawer takes about four hours. If you have hundreds of old files on your computer, it could take several more. If the peace of mind you will get from going through the items is worth hours of your time, then by all means make an appointment with yourself to do it as soon as possible. If spending that time in some other way is more important, then throw the items away immediately. If you find yourself postponing the decision, ask yourself, "What am I going to know tomorrow that I don't know today?"

Just Get Started

At this point, one of the major questions you may have is "How long will it take?" You cannot expect to solve all of your paper/document-management problems overnight. Don't worry how long it will take. One thing I know is that the longer you wait, the longer it will take, and the harder it will be! Just get started. One of the most exciting things you will discover is that what you learn in organizing one area of your life will carry over into other areas. As you enjoy your successes, it will encourage you to keep going.

Keep It Growing

There are no magic wands! No matter how terrific the system you develop, it will not maintain itself, and it will not last forever. If after reading this book, or even parts of it, you have to admit that you are not willing to do what needs to be done, then your assignment is to determine who will help you and how.

Keep in mind, however, that the key issue in any paper/document-management system is decision making. You will either have to make the decisions yourself, or give the person to whom you delegate your paper management the authority to make those decisions. A successful system will probably require a combination of decision-making and delegation.

Many times a client will call me because a system they have established is not working. Nine times out of 10, the problem is not that the system was bad but that they have outgrown the system. Personal paper management is an ongoing process. It will need to change as you change. If your priorities, your support system, your space availability or your family situation change, you may need to adjust your system to fit those changes.

Call for Action

If you have read this book and still don't know how to create an effective system or want additional support or assistance for your specific needs, you have several options. Read through this Q and A section to see what they are:

Q: I'd like to talk to you, are you available?

A: Contact me – I'd love to hear from you!

> Barbara Hemphill
> Hemphill & Associates, Inc.
> 467 Lake Eva Marie Drive
> Raleigh, NC 27603
> 800-427-0237
> www.BarbaraHemphill.com
> Barbara@BarbaraHemphill.com
> Facebook: Barbara.hemphill1
> Twitter: @barbhemphill

Q. It seems that in this age of high technology, information changes so fast. How can I stay current?

A. We frequently add updates as we become aware of them to our website, in addition to new resources, free downloadable articles, surveys and more. So, visit www.BarbaraHemphill.com often, bookmark the site, or better yet sign up for the free ezine and stay informed.

Q. Who else can help me?

A. Certified Productive Environment Specialists (CPES), are a team of productivity professionals that have undergone an extensive training program by me, to help clients get organized so they can accomplish their work and enjoy their lives. To find one in your area, go to www.ProductiveEnvironment.com.

Q. What are my other options?

A. You can check your local yellow pages or search online for "Organizing Consultants" or "Personal Services" and find someone who specializes in setting up systems for paper management. Contact NAPO (National Association for Professional Organizers) http://www.napo.net or the ICD (listed above) for a list of organizers in your area.

Q. How do I work with a consultant?

A. Many people procrastinate about making an appointment with an organizing consultant. They're often stuck with the "clean up before the maid comes" syndrome, or they are concerned about how to prepare for his or her arrival.

Put aside any worries about needing to justify your situation. The organizing consultant's role is to provide professional advice, not to make judgments. Ask yourself the questions: "Why did I make this appointment with an organizing consultant?" and "What do I want to change?"

It is not necessary to do anything, but if you feel a need to get started before the consultant comes, here are some suggestions.

- The consultant will begin work immediately, so choose where you would like to begin—with today's mail or the attic.
- Gather together any supplies you may have on hand that will be helpful in the organizing process—file folder, labels, marking pens, boxes, containers, wastebaskets, etc.
- Put all like things together—banking information, photographs, magazines, etc.
- Relax! If you're unsure about where to begin or what to do, your organizing consultant has the knowledge and experience to guide you in making that decision.

Q. What can you expect from an organizing consultant?

A. The first step in developing a good working relationship with an organizing consultant is to have a realistic understanding of what particular services that consultant offers. Although every organizing consultant is different, you can and should expect:

- Complete confidentiality.
- Open discussion about the cost of services.
- Appointments scheduled to meet your professional and/or personal needs.
- An ability to apply the "principles of organization" to your particular situation.
- Expertise and experience in the "principles of organization" applied to personal and professional life.
- Creative and innovative problem solving.

- Availability and a continued interest in your situation, should you desire.

Some organizing consultants specialize in "hands on" assistance, which may include:

- A willingness to do whatever task needs to be done in the interest of achieving mutually determined goals.
- Physical assistance, as well as verbal instruction. A willingness to do whatever you would do—including getting dirty!
- Shopping assistance if you need or want it.
- Assistance in finding another professional resource if it is appropriate or desirable.

There are hundreds of organizing consultants in the country, and more are being trained every day. The exciting aspect of the industry is the networking that takes place among the organizers themselves. Not all organizers provide the same services so keep looking until you find the one that suits your needs and your personality. If the first one you try doesn't work out, don't give up!

Q. What if it's not me that needs organizing, it's my family?

A. A Note of Caution: it is always easier to see what someone else needs to do than it is to see what we need to do ourselves. In teaching organizing skills to families, one of my key roles is to ensure that family members concentrate on solving their own organizing problems instead of what other family members need to do. As you read this book and experiment with developing new paper-management systems for yourself, resist the urge to insist that other people join you. Many of the systems you develop will automatically make paper management easier for other people, but let them discover it for themselves!

Although you are at the end of this book, you are at the beginning of a new adventure in learning to control the paper in your life. Remember, "In every organizing process, things will get worse before they get better." Try to remain optimistic. Forgive yourself when you see the mistakes you have made in the past and move on. Feeling bad about yourself does not help anything. Be willing to ask for help when you need it, and reward yourself for each accomplishment along the way. Now grab that tiger by the tail! You are on your way to a personal paper-management system that works for you. Happy organizing!

Appendix

Records Retention Guide
Throughout this book I've written about different kinds of paper that you need to keep—or might want to keep. This retention guide will serve as a quick reference tool for you to use to identify your papers, and note where you keep them and how long they need to be retained. You can write in this book, make a note of the item's location and fill out how long to keep it if you have not already included that information. Keep the chart handy.

This pullout guide is also available on my website, www.barbarahemphill.com.

In many cases, it's up to you where you want to keep a document and for how long. I've indicated a specific location and/or retention guide where this is a legal requirement—or I've felt it would be helpful to do so.

Keep in mind where you keep documents is not nearly as important as doing it consistently. Problems develop when part of the information you need is in one location and part is in another. However, because of space considerations, it may sometimes be necessary to put documents in more than one place. When this happens, be sure to note both locations. For example, old tax records could be stored in the attic while the most recent year's records could be in your reference files.

Be sure to include a timetable for transferring records from active to inactive storage or disposal. (A good time to do this would be after you file your tax return.) You may find the least complicated method for keeping records is to put all records for a given year into a large envelope or box and store them in chronological order. When you put in the latest year's records, take out unneeded or unwanted materials from earlier years.

Document	Location	Retain for How Long
Education Records		
Certificates		
Diplomas		
Letters of Reference		Update periodically
Resumes		Until superseded
Health Records		
Illness records		Permanently
Vaccination Records		Permanently
Insurance		
Auto		Statute of limitations (in case of late claims)
Disability		Duration of policy
Health		Duration of policy
Homeowner's		Statute of limitations (in case of late claims)
Liability		Statute of limitations (in case of late claims)
Life	Safe Deposit Box	Duration of policy
Personal Property		Duration of policy
Umbrella policy		Duration of policy
Investments		

Purchase records		As long as you own a security, then keep with sale record
Sales records		Six years after sale, for tax purposes
Major home improvements		As long as you own, then with tax records
Collectibles		As long as you own, then with tax records
Household inventory		Update annually
Mortgage information		Six years after sale
Military records		
Discharge papers	Keep in a safe deposit box.	Permanently
Personal-Property records		
Automobile registration	Keep copy in car, original with driver.	As long as you own auto
Receipts for major purchases		As long as you own item
Personal life		
Calendars (past)		
Directories		
Letters/greeting cards		
Memorabilia		
Photographs		

Religious records		
Tax and Financial		
Bank statements		Six years
Canceled checks		Six years, if for deductible item
Certificates of deposit		Until cashed in
Contracts		Six years after completion
Credit card statements, receipts		Six years if for deductible item
Income tax returns		Permanently
Income tax support forms, papers		Six years. Exception: Keep non-deductible IRA form indefinitely.
Loan agreements		Six years after payment
Loan payment books		Until paid
Pension plan records		Current year only
Rental contracts		As long as in effect
Pay stub		Until W2 confirmed
Trust agreements		As long as in effect
Vital Records		
Adoption papers	Safe deposit box	Permanently
Automobile title	Safe deposit box	As long as you own auto

Birth certificates	Safe deposit box	Permanently
Citizenship papers	Safe deposit box	Permanently
Copyrights, Patents	Safe deposit box	As long as in effect
Death certificates	Safe deposit box	Until estate is settled
Divorce decrees	Safe deposit box	Permanently
Marriage certificate	Safe deposit box	Permanently
Passports		Keep current
Power of attorney		Permanently. Update as needed.
Safety deposit box key		As long as you keep box
Safe deposit box inventory		As long as you keep box. Update regularly
Social Security records		Permanently
Wills		As long as valid
Warranties and instructions		**As long as you own item**

Resources

Reading
Bushido Business by Barbara Hemphill with Stephen M.R. Covey, Tom Hopkins, and Brian Tracy. Available at all major bookstores.

Good Advice Press book, Stop Junk Mail Forever. Great ways to get off mailing lists. Available at: http://www.goodadvicepress.com/sjmf.htm.

Love it or Lose It: Living Clutter Free Forever and Taming the Paper Tiger at Work both by Barbara Hemphill and available at www.barbarahemphill.com.

The Clutter Diet - Lorie Moreno's tips and ideas for losing unwanted clutter. http://www.clutterdiet.com/

Tools
Direct Marketing Association – Get your address off junk mailing lists. http://www.the-dma.org

Free Credit Report – Check your credit report with each of the three bureaus for free. https://www.annualcreditreport.com/cra/index.jsp

Productive Environment Scorecard – Find out where your organizing challenges lie. www.productiveenvironment.com

Send Out Cards – Choose, write, address and mail cards to friends, family members, clients and colleagues — all in one place. https://www.sendoutcards.com

Shoeboxed - One of the best solutions for handling business cards and receipts you collect. http://www.shoeboxed.com/

Products
Dymo Label Makers – Label makers are great way to make sure you know where to find everything. http://sites.dymo.com

Fujitsu Scan Snap Scanners – Excellent tool for scanning in papers, receipts and business cards.
http://www.fujitsu.com/us

PBWorks – An online collaboration and document writing/management tool.
http://pbworks.com

Pendaflex File Folders – Although they are more expensive, they come with a lifetime guarantee.

Planner Pads – Useful paper calendars.
http://www.plannerpads.com

The SwiftFile Solution - Eliminate the clutter on your desk or counter with these folders for each day of the month.
http://www.productiveenvironment.com/products/swiftfile-products.html

The "To Do" Book – Keep track of to-do items, receipts and more.
http://www.barbarahemphill.com/products/taming-the-paper-tiger-books

Recycling Options
Find a recycling center in your Zip code.
http://earth911.com/

Computers with Causes – Find a place that needs your old computer.
http://www.computerswithcauses.org/

About the Authors

Barbara Hemphill started her organizing career in 1978 with a $7 ad in a New York City newspaper. Today, as the founder of the Productive Environment Institute, she leads an international team of Certified Productive Environment Specialists™.

A respected expert in paper, information and time management, and work/life balance, Barbara's books include Kiplinger's Taming the Paper Tiger series, Love It or Lose It: Living Clutter-Free Forever, Bushido Business, co-authored by Stephen M.R. Covey, Tom Hopkins, and Brian Tracy, and her 2011 release, Organizing Paper @Home: What to Toss and How to Find the Rest.

Spanning a 30-year career on the cutting edge of a growing industry, Barbara has appeared on the Today Show and Good Morning America, in Reader's Digest, USA Today, Kiplinger's Personal Finance, The New York Times, Real Simple, and Guideposts magazine. She is past president of the National Association of Professional Organizers, a winner of the Founder's Award, and a two-time winner of the President's Award.

An adventurer as well as an innovator, Barbara has lived in the West Indies, India, New York City, and Washington, DC. While living in India in the 1970's, she adopted three orphaned children. In addition, her family includes two stepchildren, four grandchildren, and her beloved one-of-a-kind husband Alfred Taylor, with whom she shares their own Productive Environment™ near Raleigh, NC.

Barbara Hemphill
Hemphill & Associates, Inc.
www.barbarahemphill.com
467 Lake Eva Marie Drive
Raleigh, NC 27603
800-427-0237
Barbara@BarbaraHemphill.com
Facebook: Barbara.hemphill1
Twitter: @barbhemphill

Jennifer Wig is a writer, editor and a professional organizer.

She started her career as a print journalist and earned several awards for her work before switching to TV news, working as a web and broadcas producer for a Raleigh television news station. In 2010, Jennifer left news to start her own business, The Final Drafts, which provides writing, editing and media relations services to individuals and small businesses. She also became a professional organizer, and met Barbara while inquiring about a career in that field. Jennifer is a member of the National Association of Professional Organizers and of the Institute for Challenging Disorganization.

She lives in Raleigh with her fiancée.

Jennifer Wig
The Final Drafts
http://thefinaldrafts.com
jennifer@jenniferwig.com
Facebook: thefinaldrafts
Twitter: @wiggitywack